Kaleidoscope

Kaleidoscope

DAVID JAFFIN

First published in the United Kingdom in 2019 by
Shearsman Books
50 Westons Hill Drive
Emersons Green
Bristol BS16 7DF

Shearsman Books Ltd Registered Office
30–31 St. James Place, Mangotsfield, Bristol BS16 9JB
(this address not for correspondence)

www.shearsman.com

ISBN 978-1-84861-639-4

Distributed for Shearsman Books in the U. S. A.
by Small Press Distribution, 1341 Seventh Avenue, Berkeley, CA 94710
E-Mail orders@spdbooks.org
www.spdbooks.org

Production, composition, & cover design: Edition Wortschatz,
a service of Neufeld Verlag, Cuxhaven/Germany
E-Mail info@edition-wortschatz.de, www.edition-wortschatz.de

Title photograph:
Hannelore Bäumler, München

Printed in Germany

Contents

9

10

13

15

17

With continuing thanks for
Marina Moisel
preparing
this manuscript

and to Hanni Bäumler
for her well-placed photograph

If I had to classify my poetry, it could best be done through the classical known "saying the most by using the least". The aim is thereby set: transparency, clarity, word-purity. Every word must carry its weight in the line and the ultimate aim is a unity of sound, sense, image and idea. Poetry, more than any other art, should seek for a unity of the senses, as the French Symbolists, the first poetic modernists, realized through the interchangeability of the senses: "I could hear the colors of her dress." One doesn't hear colors, but nevertheless there is a sensual truth in such an expression.

Essential is "saying the most by using the least". Compression is of the essence. And here are some of my most personal means of doing so turning verbs into nouns and the reverse, even within a double-context "Why do the leaves her so ungenerously behind". Breaking words into two or even three parts to enable both compression and the continuing flow of meaning. Those words must be placed back together again, thereby revealing their inner structure-atomising.

One of my critics rightly said: "Jaffin's poetry is everywhere from one seemingly unrelated poem to the next." Why? Firstly because of my education and interests trained at New York University as a cultural and intellectual historian. My doctoral dissertation on historiography emphasizes the necessary historical continuity. Today we often judge the past with the mind and mood of the present, totally contrary to their own historical context. I don't deny the past-romanticism and classical but integrate them within a singular modern context of word-usage and sensibility. Musically that would place me within the "classical-romantic tradition" of Haydn, Mozart, Mendelssohn, Brahms and Nielsen but at the very modern end of that tradition.

My life historically is certainly exceptional. My father was a prominent New York Jewish lawyer. The law never interested me, but history always did. A career as a cultural-intellectual historian was mine-for-the-asking, but I rejected historical relativism. That led me to a marriage with a devout German lady – so I took to a calling of Jesus-the-Jew in post-Auschwitz Germany. For ca. two decades I wrote and lectured all over Germany on Jesus the Jew. Thereby my knowledge and understanding of both interlocked religions became an essential part of my being. History, faith and religion two sides of me but also art, classical music and literature were of essential meaning – so many poems on poetry, classical music and painting.

Then Rosemarie and I have been very happily married for 57 years now. Impossible that a German and Jew could be so happily married so shortly after the war? I've written love poems for her, hundreds and hundreds over those 57 years, not only the love poems, as most are, of the first and often unfulfilling passion, but "love and marriage go together like a horse and carriage". Perhaps too prosaic for many poets?

When did I become a poet? My sister Lois wrote reasonably good poetry as an adolescent. I, only interested in sports until my Bar Mitzvah, a tournament tennis and table-tennis player, coached baseball and basketball teams, also soccer.

My sister asked whether I'd ever read Dostoyevsky.
I'd only read John R. Tunis sports books and the
sports section of the *New York Times* so I answered
"in which sports was he active?" She said, rather con-
descendingly, "If you haven't read Dostoyevsky, you
haven't lived." So I went to the library for the very
first time and asked for a book by this Dostoyevsky.
I received *Poor People*, his first book, that made him
world famous. My mother shocked to see me reading
and most especially a book about poor people said,
"David, don't read that it will make you sad, unhappy
– we, living in Scarsdale, weren't after all, poor peo-
ple. From there it went quickly to my Tolstoy, Hardy
and so on. In music it started with the hit parade, then
Lost in the Stars, then the popular classics and with 15
or 16 my Haydn, Mozart, Schütz, Victoria ... And
then at Ann Arbor and NYU to my artists, most es-
pecially Giovanni Bellini, Van der Weyden, Georges
de la Tour, Corot and Gauguin ...

But it was Wallace Stevens' reading in the early 50s
in the YMHA that set me off – he didn't read very
well, but his 13 Ways of Looking at a Blackbird, Idea
of Order at Key West, Two Letters (in *Poems Posthu-
mous*), Peter Quince at the Clavier, The Snowman ...
and the excellent obituary in *Time* magazine plus the
letter he answered some of my poems with compli-
ments but "you must be your own hardest critic".
That pre-determined my extremely self-critical way
with a poem. Please don't believe that prolific means
sloppy, for I'm extremely meticulous with each and
every poem.

My poems are published in the order written and I'm way ahead of any counting ... The poem is a dialogical process as everything in life. The words come to me not from me, and if they strike or possibly join-a-union then I become desparate, read long-winded poets like Paz to set me off – he's very good at odd times. Those poems need my critical mood-mind as much as I need its very specially chosen words – not the "magic words" of the romantics, but the cleansed words of Jaffin – Racine used only 500 words. My words too are a specially limited society, often used, but in newly-felt contexts.

O something very special: I have a terrible poetic memory. If I had a good one as presumably most poets, I'd write say one poem about a butterfly, and every time I see/saw a butterfly it would be that one, that poem. But I forget my poems, so each butterfly, lizard, squirrel ... is other-placed, other-mooded, other-worded, other-Jaffined. That's the main reason why I am most certainly the most prolific of all poets.

Shakespeare is the greatest of us: his sonnets live most from the fluency and density of his language. I advise all future poets to keep away from his influence and the poetic greatness of The Bible.

Yours truly
David Jaffin

P. S.: As a preacher the truth (Christ) should become straight-lined, timelessly so, but as a poet it's quite different. What interests me most are those contraditions which live deeply within all of us, not only in theory, but daily in the practice. And then the romantics have led me to those off-sided thoroughly poetic truths that mysteriously not knowing where that darkened path will lead us.

The pier

    remind

    s me of ab
    sent-minded

    persons whose
    reveries

    stopped some
    where in the

    middle of a
    nowhere from

    finding-on.

The castle

    near Hagenau

    now only in
    habited with

    the window
    s of why

    time has left
    it with those

    centurie
    s of lost re

    membrance
    s.

She

never grew

out of be
ing what she

always was
a perenn

ial flower
in search of

change
able color

s.

Flat mo

ments the
lake level

ed down to
a common

place of per
sonal expos

ures.

The boat

increas

ing my mind a
float with

the waves of
transient im

pression
s.

The intima

cies of spring–

time tree
s faint

ly leafed
though bare

ly confid
ing.

Lindau

gracious

ly tower
ing over a

past harbour
ed secure

ly in the
breath of

sun-down
ed appear

ances.

Snow

in the dis

tance cool
ing the wind

s into a
night of

contempla
tive shadow

ings.

On guard

One can'

t be on–
guard even

from one
self no pro

tective
shield only

a naked bare
ness from

the severity
of its wound

s timefully
scarred.

Why the winds change

Is it why

the winds
change dir

ections to
time us in

to those re
newing phases

of its over–
coming truth

s.

That late Corot

heard so

finely
through the

transpar
encies of

voice
less shadow

ings.

Saint-Saëns

composed

so fluent
ly that his

ear often
voiced so

tasteless
ly appar

ent.

From Meersburg to Lindau

This lake'

s surround
ing my thought

s with the
width of its

soothing-
surfaced

enclosure
s.

Even poem

s fleshed–
in time-im

pending si
lence

s.

a) Dvorak's

Quartet op. 105
scherzo

uplifting a
peasant's em

phatically-
souled dance-

calling
s.

b) Reicha'

s wind music
polishes–up

silver-illum
inating per

spective
s.

c) Janacek'

s 1st Quartet
pregnantly

tensing a uni
fying disassem

bling other
wiseness.

a) Each day

weeks–now
repetitive

ly–samed
futureless

waiting
s.

b) Sketched

bare-line
trees scarce

ly inhabit
ing their

vacantly-
implied

silence
s.

a) As the Judaic Law

How tight
did that young

dog need-to-
be-leashed

from his in
stinctual–

urging
s.

b) Poetic translations

That stand–
by ladder

stood motion
lessly to the

invasive
height of its

bi-lingual
poetic-trans

lation
s.

c) Color blind

ness as a pro
tective shield

against
too-brightly

provocative
intensitie

s.

d) How can

one bridge
the torrent

ial current
s of spring'

s mountain
ously-avowed

releasing
s.

e) Ives' unanswer

ed question e
vasively e

choing back.

a) Something

missing a sense
of lost spac

ed–silence
s.

b) He stood

at the height
of distanc

ing no–where
s–else but

then.

c) The night

as a tidal
sea of in

dwelling bey
ondness.

d) Why ask

for more
when now'

s the only
time–held mo

ment.

e) "It is ful

filled" as if
He'd bodied

those last
thirsting–

claim
s.

f) Why did

he fear the
depth of an

all–preclud
ing sadness.

g) When the

stars light-
redeeming

that time
less void

of his.

h) Does touch

envision
more than the

word's fail
ing breadth.

i) Stilled curr

ents winter'
s dry-veined

death-grasp
ings.

j) Rosemarie

only the two
of our inse

parably-sens
ed loneli

ness.

k) As those

birds left be
hind the o

ther side of
the mountain

ously intense-
pursuing warm

th-calling
s.

l) Why ask

for the more
of what's

still incom
pletely now.

Stars dens

>ing the heaven
>s with unanswer
>
>ing light-pre
>ception
>
>s.

The heavy

>fogs seemed
>to obscure
>
>time as float
>ing impress
>
>ions scarce
>ly realized.

Te Deum in D *(Zelenka)*

>Can music be
>come more
>
>brightly en
>lightened
>
>than this
>pulsing through
>
>a faith irre
>vocably self–
>
>certained.

Family Portrait

They posed
an indelible

image of what
should-have-

been thorough
ly self-satis

fying.

a) Kafka'

s Prague Jew-
dead now street

ed with little
more than se

ductive over-
night tempta

tions.

b) Kafka as

Roth prophet
ically inhab

ited with
those dead-

down time
s evilly breed

ing apocalypt
ic first war'

s time's-end.

c) If only

the touch of
a transpar

ently scent
ed rose could

reawaken time'
s withholding

awareness
es.

d) When night'

s light-trans
parent dark

nesses seem e
vanescent

ly impress
ionistic.

Personae (6)

a) This orna

mental carpet
brightly im

pressed with
intricate

ly pre-design
ed phrasing

s.

b) Car light

s owl-eying
through night'

s time-resist
ant uncertain

ties.

c) He appear

ed cactused
with the de

sert's light-
thirsting

thistle
s.

d) As that Peiss

er fox lumin
osly-entren

ched darkly-
unfathom

ed.

e) Those un

earthly fog
s dissolv

ing into a
transcend

ing light-
appearance.

f) A lonely

road wooded
in irresol

ute time-con
suming

s.

a) Sound

proof moment
s at the

sea's bottom
ed sanctuar

ies.

b) The eye-of-

the–storm depth
ed witness

ing the where
of nowhere

s–else.

c) Force

ful poem
s intens

ing a quiet
ly restrain

ed form–in
tent.

d) The classi

cal bright
ness of Beet

hoven's Wald
stein Sonata

darkly-demoni
cally light-

clashing.

e) The quiet

after-the-
storm's time

lessly self-
withholding.

f) Why need-

envision dark
vistas when

fear's at the
inside-out

of our time-
ripening

gladness
es.

g) Innocent

children
skipping un

evened stone'
s balanc

ing aware
nesses.

h) "The rest

is (the) si
lence" of Shakes

peare's blood-
thirsting

drama
s.

i) When winter

ed birds assume
a branch-sett

ling composur
ed restless

ness.

j) When she

died that
room still en

compassing
her feared

untouch
able silen

ces.

k) Why need

of monumen
tal phrasing

s when the
mountain'

s time-breed
ing its re

clusive shad
owing

s.

l) They sat

their life'
s end-out

windowing
a timeless

reach.

m) Who can en

vision the
horizoned

darkening
reaches' sun–

setting.

n) For Rosemarie

whose smile
melts mount

ains of my
own dire

steadfast
ness.

a) Listen

ing to the
frequenc

es of time'
s rhythmic

ally residual
instinctual

awareness
es.

b) What could

have been now
restlessly

reassuring
time's even-

steadied rhy
thmic flow.

c) Pre-deter

mined despite
our willful

ly devious
routing those

spontaneous
mapped-out

self-certain
ties?

d) as a bird

nesting its

own instinct
ual home-find

ings

e) or that I'

ve-been-here-
before feel

ing refresh
ing as one'

own newly-
discovered re-

painted house.

f) Pink may

have changed
clothes prompt

ly self-assum
ing according

to time and
season their

closeted left–
behind

s.

g) Time-for-

flight the
wander-bird

s empty-
skied practis

ing their wing
èdly adept

initiative
s.

h) Was it

the voice of
that time-im

pending ri
ver calling

its distant
ly refrain

ed

i) or the aut

umnal death-re
viving color-

disguised hori
zoned-vast

ness.

j) Rosemarie

let us take
hands now to

their instin
ctively intell

ing less-
than-this.

a) Snowless

time's bare-
ground remem

brance of
that empty-

faced silen
ce.

b) Windstill

not even a
bird shadow

lessly sens
ed.

c) This room

furnished
with lamp

lit contem
plation

s.

d) Why have

all these
trees been

stripped-
down of

their dense
ly-leafed

shadow
ings.

e) You can't

kill the dead
they're still

inhabiting
every inch

of this room'
s time–spac

ing.

a) It's the

words that
tell chosen

to their own
self–satisfy

ing cause

b) not those

warmth rever
ied–feeling

s overcom
ing a stead

fast–inert
ia

c) or the i

dea of the
thing itself

untoucha
bly elusive

d) (though)

open-ending
silence

s spacial
ly unresolv

ing

e) a poem'

s predeter
mining self–

sufficien
cy.

f) Why need

of more than
the taste

of fresh
fruit's re

freshing
ly thirst

ing

g) or the sin

gular touch
of a rose

increasing
ly colored

to its own
articulate

intent.

h) Those own

scarcely un
remember

ed moment
s that life

our realiz
ed together

ness.

i) He felt-

down to the
depthed–claim

s of that
mountain'

s immovable
growth.

j) The lei

sure of a
summer day'

s shading
inclusive

self–satis
fying appear

ance
s.

k) Why ask

for more
only now the

word's self–
evident

cleanli
ness appeal

s.

"Serioso Quartet" *(Beethoven op 95)*

Defiant mus

ic rhythmical
ly attaca as

if lyrical
beauty had be

come (short
breathed) but

a secondary
recourse.

a) He felt

(at time
s) as a mis

placed person
catching-up

at wasn't his
indigenous

ly becoming.

b) Chameleon-

like (almost
seasonally)

change-of-
colors as if

personed to
a no-where

s-else.

c) Could he

have imagined
(if imagin

ed at all)
the 16 year-

old out-of-
step from "him

self" shadow
ing such an

untimely lone
liness.

d) Or the "Jew

ish minister"
preaching

at the height
of that dead-

ground's
bottomless

fall.

e) At 77 now

unquieting
the night'

s comfort
ing silence

s with such
a poetic–necess

ity.

f) Had love

or that un
known call

ing voiced–
it all-time

s past-time
s.

Night-time'

s shadow
less aware

ness the
moon's un

seen presen
ce irresist
ably alive.

The image

before His
voiced time–

unifying
creation

ed.

Can those im

pulsing curr
ents (however

mountain
ously intend

ing) rhy
thmical

ly ceased e
ven at winter'

s deadly-de
termining

intent.

a) A garden

ed view o
pened-us-out

to its light-
encompass

ings.

b) We listen

ed intently
to the sea'

s invoking
imagin

ings.

c) Light glass-

reflecting
momentary

touched–trans
parencie

s.

d) Rosemarie

what need
for more than

these sound
less intima

cies.

Classical

taste's sens
ing more reali

zing less.

As sky-

felt bird
s instinct

ively evok
ing these dis

tant calls of
no-wheres-

else.

Contrasts (4)

a) Fauré

s Requiem'
s sweet-same

nesses as a
tropical

fruit's per
fume-light

taste-find
s.

b) Haydn castl

ed in remote
distancing

s pre-rout
ing those in

evitable
time-rhythm

ic instinct
s-of-his.

c) Beethoven'

s seldom
hold–low

on his emot
ive source–e

ruption
s.

d) Those Christ

mas–Advent
songs English

or German
awakening

such distant
ly evoking

longing
s.

a) Buttoned

tight to a
prim sense

of prettily
withhold

ing exposure
s.

b) Turkish

oval eye
s that spoke

of intimate
ly infold

ing proced
ures.

c) Tempting

ly reveal
ing more of

those
fruit-ripe

squeezed-
down sensed-

appeal
s.

d) More the

exquisite
length of

bodied-i
magin

ings.

Quartet op 18,1 *(Beethoven)*

insistent
ly there e

ven before
a breath

ed–down
paused–mo

ment.

a) Dulled

winter's motion
less dream

ed–shadow
ings.

b) Not even a

random bird

could tempor
arily upset

those sleep–
sensed silen

ces.

c) Why wait

for what's un
expectedly

time-rehear
sing.

d) Even the

berries seem
punctuating

voiceless
coloring

s.

Akhmatova (10)

a) Tasteful

descriptive
personal

but where'
s that some

thing more
abstract word–

competence
that marks–

off a way a
part as snow

freshly–fall
en distinct
ly–aware.

b) a kind of

woman sensi
tivity of that

"glad to know
you" but why

the snow has
n't deeper-fall

en indistinct
ly unfathom

ed.

c) Fet

often yes
but not con

sistent
ly so a fine

aesthetic
at its best

distinctive
ly short–

breathed.

d) Translation

s Can a poem
really live a

gain languag
ed to a bridge

that at time
s appears arti

ficially
cross-river

s.

e) I wonder

if Jaffin in
French Spanish

or German say
s-the-same

off-direct
ioned yet some

how other
wise-voiced.

f) 2nd Command

ment (Moses)

Are we per

petually en
dangered

recreating
other's poem

s in the in
delible image

of our own.

g) Does a lang

uage (this or

that) change
the quality

of a poem
its own

personal
ly-sourced

say-so
s.

h) If each

poem in the
midst of a

personal
here-time

d no-where
s-else.

i) like the mus

ic we hear
between the be

fore and a
fterward

s – other
wise

j) that same

black bird
roof-topp

ed imperson
ally distinct

yet not the–
now of yester

day.

Big man

big car
big sense

stream-lin
ed of be

ing big.

a) Winter dark

ness only as
deep as that

withholding
sense of not–

knowing-where.

b) Soundless

appearance
the moon

voiced in
snow–crystall

ed enlighten
ings.

Northern Elegies *(Akhmatova)*

suddenly a
live to the

death–spell
s that poem

us into
those last

ing depth
s of forget

fulness.

The Star of

Bethlehem Rhein
berger's late

romantic
more-so as a

cake cream-
layered to o

vereaten full
nesses.

St. Saens'

Christmas Story
lyrically-harp

ed to such
heavenly

sweetness
es choric-an

gelic Christ
mas blessing

s.

Sprotte (2)

a) color-enrapt

ured wave-
free from his

copy-fine
Renaiss

ance-like in
delible port

raiture.

b) Sprotte at

his best time
s the field

s singing
their fine

ly appraised
spring-phras

ings.

Akhmatova

oft person-
poet place-

time discurs
ively self–

attuning.

a) Vietnam 1945

(for Chung)

French–Japan
ese–Chinese

down to the
hungered

rest–remain
s of a no–

wheres self–
finding

space left.

b) Vietnam'

s perpetuat
ing identity–

crisis classi
cally Confuc

ian–astute
ly modern

modes on–and–
off cloth

ed.

c) If there'

s one identi
ty left the

land itself
continual

ly refashion
ed as a wo

man many-lov
ed however

fictive
ly un–samed.

Pirandello'

s inner–recall
ing psychol

ogically ad
ept (though
improbably

reassur
ing) sensed–

of–humour.

December-

>   times these
>   dreary-cold
>
>   all-consum
>   ing days to
>
>   a blanked-
>   out self-con
>
>   sciousness.

The bird out

>   spreading its
>   wide wing
>
>   s self-enclos
>   ing the re
>
>   luctant
>   ly night-lit
>
>   town below.

Bassett

>   hound heavier
>   than his
>
>   weight could
>   carry eyes de
>
>   serts of un
>   timely expos
>
>   ures.

Ravel's

Quartet's sun–
lit reverie

s indwell
ing mood-shad

owing
s.

Seemed (15)

a) Shy he

seemed to
appear under

things not
quite surfac

ing to the
full impact

of his own
unsteadied

self.

b) Ravel'

s Quartet
at times

seemed as
if open-air

ed to shad
owless fa

çade
s.

c) French poet

ic symbolism
seems to "under

stand" the in
timacies of

sensed–imaged–
impulsing

s as if tenta
tively voic

ing its own
self–appear

ance
s.

d) She mask

ed untold
though intang

ibly sky–
floating dis

tancing
s.

e) Does the mo

mentary un
said often

appear weight
lessly un

assuming.

f) A shadow

ed world
though ines

capably time-
secluding.

g) Why do

your eye
s seem to

sea–me in
to waved

transpar
encie

s.

h) Why re

veal what ap
pears time

lessly self–
conceal

ing.

i) Monet'

s self-awak
ening shadow

less bright
nesses.

j) That moon-

sensed whis
pered echo

less re
sponse.

k) Redon-like

they sail
ed tight

ly-tacked
beyond un

timed wind-
kept sea

scape
s.

l) He hid-away

from his
own self-poss

essing claim
s.

m) Lithe branch

es nakedly
numbed wind–

escaping win
ter's menac

ing call.

n) Window

ed transparen
cies left them

but shadow
ing inescap

able silenc
es.

o) The fabric

of her dress
es worn-down

feeling
s of past-

time social
pleasure

s.

These fall

en leave
s have left

a forsaken
emptiness

deep-down
at his heart'

s once-felt
lowering

sensibili
ties.

a) "David's

poems are
better than

himself"
as if art

(as love
and faith)

transform
ing beyond

the shadow
ing realm

s of self-pre
cluding dark

nesses.

b) St. Peter

walked–upon
the–waves

only as long
as Christ'

s calling
kept–him–

there upbal
ancing.

c) Rosemarie'

s beauty con
tinuously

illuminate
s those dark

ly-sensed
dominion

s of my
own.

d) His once

errant boat
guided by a

distant sig
nalling glow

passed through
those night-

indwelling
danger-zone

s.

e) As Akhmatova

wrote of Russia'
s past histor

ies though al
ways safely at

tuned to those
of her own

constantly
threaten

ed being.

f) Even autumn'

s death-trans
forming a

brightness
vividly a

flame with
its allusive

ly beautify
ing scent.

g) Why (for

those faithed–
in-Christ)

fear death'
s ultimate

ly fruit
less claim

s-on-us.

h) Dostoyev

sky arrested
with evil

spirits still
out-lived

spiritual
ly-intact

their perpet
uating claim

s-on-him.

i) These self-

same word
s derive a

cleansing
fitness a

self-defin
ing blue-sk

ied clarity.

j) Rosemarie

is our self-
transcend

ing love
but faint

ly imaging
a-life-of

the-world
to-come.

a) This sky'

s become
leafless

ly forebod
ing.

b) Pass

ages of the
mind tunnel

ed in obscur
ed darkness

es.

c) A snow

less December
the ground'

s become hard
and exposed

as a woman
loveless

ly vacant.

d) as a boat

sailing the
restless

quiet of
stilled wat

ers.

e) Akhmatova

1921

The distan

cing loss
throbbing

love's pain
ed-close

ness to
then.

a) "Hommage à

Sprotte"

Are we all (Constable/
willingly

or not)
sourced in a

tradition
that make

s more-of-
us than we

can realize
why.

b) Or are

some but epi
gons of too–

much other
wise–than–

self.

c) Some (espec

ially today)

cult the so–
called "orig

inal" because
they're so–

much–in–need
of a mirror

less self–re
cognition.

d) Does true

art continue
to voice–its–

own surpris
ingly signif

ied as our
name–sake

if only for
appearance–

sake.

e) Are we

(then) but

craftsmen
of a pre-

given instin
ct at the in

terior depth
s of our in

visibly wit
nessing

self.

f) The sky

cloud-invok
ing appear

ed moving
beyond his

own shadow
ing self.

g) The ever-

appealing
night woke

him to what
needed a

word-imaged
companion-

guide.

h) If it'

s not writt
en to its

pre-appear
ing self a

void ineff
ably felt −

estranged.

i) Why listen

(even momentar
ily sensed)

to what'
s pre-assum

ing these
landscaped

self-shadow
ings.

j) What must-

be-said re
mains indelib

ly written
and conceiv

ed for its-
own-sake.

Father and daughter (3)

a) Sly as a

fox instinct
ively oblique

she could
steal your well–

meaning away
hide it in

her closet of
pocketed

jewel
s.

b) Two-faced

a behind–the–
back kind of

person secret
ly self–in

dulging his
otherwise

smiling–af
fects.

c) Sick'

s a nicer
psycho-word

white-wash
ing their en

demmic pre
valence for

evil-intent
ions.

a) She seem

ed as if
double-imag

ed focusing
though ob

scurely in
tent.

b) A city of

snow-dream
s as if

timeless
ly self-in

tending.

c) Akhmatova

the only sur
vivor poetiz

ing that
lost-time-

sensed city.

d) He became

wooded dense
ly inhabit

ing those
dreamed-se

quencie
s.

e) When pain

becomes too
intense to

heal its
penetrat

ing calling
s.

f) Why try

to imagine
what's be

come illus
ively dimm

ed timeless
ly uneas

ing.

g) That vacant

unknown church
reclining

its soft-
down stead

ied contem
plation

s.

h) Neil contin

ues to remem
ber my self-

escaping
fictive mo

ments.

i) Is time

though illu
sively–sensed

still but
rain–shadow

ing.

j) Those moon-

imitating
kites heaven

ly light–re
assuring.

k) River mirr

oring its in
stinctive

ly reveried
reflection

s.

l) The invis

ible wind'
s self-illum

inating time
less expanse

s.

a) Mandelstam'

s poems made
me feel famil

iar his imag
ed time-plac

ed eluding
sensibil

ities.

b) He disapp

eared as so
many other

s into a
vastly undis

covered obliv
ion.

a) Phantom

voices in the
night neither

here or there
but still re

taining their
invisible

power
s.

b) He possess

ed those trans
cient eye

s of an hab
itual self-de

ceiver.

c) That fear

as an untouch
able person

mutely re
solving

though still
increasing

ly present.

d) Why shad

ow oneself
when dark

ness remain
s perpetual

ly overcom
ing.

e) That "con

fidence man"
as in "Othello"

secretly whis
pering untouch

able desire
s.

f) Once mirr

oring his
tentative

face momen
tarily

voice-chang
ing.

g) When ghost

s of a former
age awakened

to haunt his
biographi

cal intent
ions.

h) Desert

ed ship
floating the

unremember
ed waves of

elusively
distant

shore
s.

i) When time

stopped in
that lonely

uninhabit
ed house

All those
once-intun

ed clock
s intent

ly self-with
holding.

j) When she

died he be
gan to live

a myth of
itself dia

logued though
ever-so-stran

gely voiced.

k) When those

self-repeat
ing wave

s become time
lessly ob

scured.

l) Distant

woods higher
treed than

the utmost
reach of his

untouchab
ly shadow

ing thought
s.

m) His mother'

s death-en
trancing

face star
ing back his

most unobed
ient past.

n) That night

moon-darken
ing the life

less image
of her help

lessly very-
presence.

a) Mandelstam'

s "Tristia
poems" (as the

late Celan) be
coming al

most untouch
ably subjective

self-entwin
ing.

b) The horse-

ridden tempi
of Mandelstam'

s longer poem
s hysterical

ly diffusely–
imaged hard–

times.

a) À la Croce

Whatever
kind of ugli

ness (however
potently real

ized) cannot
subdue my

beautify
ing over–tim

ed evoking–
sensibili

ties.

b) À la Keats

Unbeautifi

ed truths as
untruthful

beauties
may dilemma

an off-bal
anced artis

tic world e
villy-sourc

ed.

My prosaic

mother penny-
pinched for

ice-cream
sodas wombed

me (neverthe
less) thorough

ly birthed-
for-poem

s.

Squirrel

s grow up–
the-tree

s flavoured
with the summar

izing taste
of nut–big

nesses.

Ugly can

only take–on
a kind of

beautify
ing spirit

ually–present
while wrinkled–

designed.

a) Small thing

s even the
should–have–

been–forgott
en edged his

time–spend
ing soul–

qualm
s.

b) Should

this or should
that those un

eased though
time-seclud

ing after-re
flection

s.

c) Confession

al soul-rang
ing dialogue

s between
the "I and

thou" person
ed in the

sameness
of those Amos

ian time-tilt
ing scale

s.

d) If only

sleep could
numb even

darken-out
those still a

wakened un
certain

ies.

e) "Out-on-

a–limb" as
a bird's

first–flight
securing

for wingèd
self-appeal

s.

f) When that

"out-of-hand"
feeling for a

quieting
steadied

safe–ground
hold.

g) Darkness

suddenly vis
ible preclud

ing all those
safety self–

impending re
assurance

s.

h) Without

you an immeas
urably insol

vent abyss.

i) Can the

dead still
lay-claim

s on our
living con

science-stric
ken reapprais

als.

j) Pink so

certained a
gainst immin

ent danger
s walled-him

self in moat-
deep impene

trable castl
ed-enclosure

s.

k) Why do

these autumn
al flight-

stricken
birds shadow

ing his so
very time-as

suming pre
sence.

l) Even that

self-perpetu
ating rose

you window-
silled to my

daily precept
ions wither

ed-down to
its lifeless

ly intold
there-being.

On Stadtfeld's "piano" recital (6)

a) F sharp minor

Toccata Bach BWV

910

Only these

persistent
under-current

waves can real
ize the accumu

lating strength
of the sea'

s unapproach
ably depthed–

silence
s.

b) Slow move

ments spaced

to the vast

skied–reach
of time's

withholding
source.

c) Can the

piano however

strongly

voiced fully
accomodate

the organ'
s consuming

orchestral
ocean

ed–depth
s.

d) Schumann'

s Toccata op 7

as if the
finger'

s ceaseless
ly intent

virtuosity
could re

place its in
creasing

need for un
touched sensi

bilitie
s.

e) Schumann'

s Humoresque

op 20

Too long

to intent a
compelling

unity of
sound-phras

ings.

f) as if feel

inged-sensitiv

ity could re

place those
Bachian form–

aspiring con
templation

s.

a) Is Tolstoy'

s most-touch

ing "Father
Martin" also

an autobio
graphical Chris

tus-like self-
redeeming

fable.

b) Tolstoy'

s Anna Karen
ina-like self–

inscented snow–
down martyr

dom at the
loving hand

s of his
wife's quiet

ly (almost
stoically) trans

forming help
lessness.

c) Had Tolstoy

become seduc
ed by the

self-grand
eur of his

pseudo-prophet
ic pose.

For Rosemarie

Semi-precious
stones however

naturally color
ed ornament

her modest
ly unassuming

self-being.

a) For a friend

who's neither
poetically-

involved Christ
ian musical

ly-intuned or
artistical

ly tasteful.

b) One must

wait-with-her
for an e

lusive comm
on-ground

to not slip-
down her polem

ically-greased
heighten

ing pole.

a) Pasternak's

verse only
snatches of

here-and-no
wheres-else i

magery.

b) I can't

follow (if I
only wanted)

his crucial
mustering

s of blind
alleyway

s.

Some of

Hesse's late
romantic autumn

al poems deep
ly coloured

lastingly
true.

a) If there'

s no other
way than that

pre-chosen
pathed through

a thicket
densely thorn

ed a no-way
s-out.

b) He kept

to the assign
ed routes of

his father's
fathers but

times had
changed their

certained
self-expos

ing continu
ity.

c) More than

once he mirr
ed himself

(though safe
ly confin

ing) other
wise.

d) The war so

changed his
very-being

that not e
ven his still-

securing wife
Penelope-

like could re
cognize his

disabled feat
ures.

e) Once in a

moment-of–
fear his home

seemed so com
pletely foreign

ed from his
self-accustom

ed eye-touch.

f) Only after

wards when it
became too

late to turn
back did he

realize his
usual train

had been rout
ed to a cause

otherwise
than his own.

g) Exiled

to strange
faces a

strange peo
ple-language

that exposed
his readied

lips to a
perpetual

silence.

h) Doris lost

her way from
our aging mo

ther's expect
ations sat

long on the
abandoned

road-side.

i) His poem

s (so famil
iar at first)

slowly be
gan to lose

their pre-
designed

face-form
s.

j) Hamlet

(for Chung)

wondered
at a world

so vastly
depthed in

mysterious
ly self-with

holding shad
owing

s.

k) Reverie

s of a snow
less winter

drifting wave
s of enlight

ened shadow
ings.

l) Last dried

fruit hang

ing down
their face

lessly intent
remembranc

es.

m) She curtain

ed her untold
pleasure

s into se
cluded realm

s of silen
ce.

a) It's only the

scholar "who
becomes what

he reads" or
perhaps a di

dactic poet
such as W. H.

b) It wasn't

the wind he
felt so soft

ly skin-phras
ing but its

invisibly
not yet time-

proven source.

c) A bird

flew in her

room one
day or was

it that insist
ant need for

her colored
bird-book with

just those
same wingèd–

approval
s.

a) Late autumn

al buds pos
ing rained–

down branch
es' self-satis

fying near
ly-voiced.

b) Brodsky

however
thoughtful

ly-sensed at
times over–

steps that
invisibly

lined poet
ic–prose.

c) Dryly-scent

ed roses

spent of
their life-

reviving
source.

d) Off-white

houses though
still impli

citly snow-
timed.

Claude Lorrain

often leaves

me with an
artificial

neo-classi
cal after-

taste where
as Constable

remains deep
ly grounded

in darkly im
mersing mood-

design
s.

a) When Brodsky

as Mandelstam

left the illum
inating shadow

s of "what
could have

been" behind
to their dull-

stamped every
day prosaical

ly Nobel Prize
qualifying

verse.

b) When poetry

as the autumn
al leaves be

comes stripped
of its sound–

colouring ex
pressive

ness Nothing
left not e

ven windless
death–dried

exposure
s.

a) If these

heavy stone
s could speak

of such time-
sensed resound

ing silence
s.

b) Tiny bird

s barely left
their tenta

tively
reflect

ive impress
ions snow-

touched.

c) The tower

ing height
of these im

mensely stat
ured building

s timeless
ly shadow

ing.

d) Continu

ous oncoming
waves phased

the shore'
s evened-out

answering
s.

e) Lamp-

light's re
flective

ly-sensed
darkness

es.

f) Why ask

of the butter
flie's flurr

ied leaf-de
fining expan

ses.

g) Rows-of-

books lined
his time-ex

tending o
ver-reach.

h) Depthed

in the night'
s weightless

ly momentary
fear-shadow

ings.

i) She felt

somehow deep
ly sourced

his eye'
s ever-tell

ing presen
ce.

j) Can the

dead overhear
their flower

ing grave'
s steadily

purifying
phrasing

s.

k) Florida'

s rehearsing
beaches im

pression
ed his on

coming
flight–feel.

l) Why dream

of that dis
tantly entran

cing rose–
scent when

the moon'
s light's

steadily pre–
conceiving.

m) For Chung

Only living
between two

worlds real
izes our depth

ed-transcend
ing other

wiseness.

n) For Neil

Home-place
became for

him just
short-time

satisfy
ing.

o) For Ingo

at the brink
of death's

releasing
closeness

over-timed
self-reveal

ing.

a) Brodskyes

que (poetized)

Left behind

day before
the day as

cends its
pre-attend

ing height
a wordless

ly self-in
voking noth

ing-less-
than-this.

b) Morning'

s lithe-branch
ed echoing

a nymph na
kedly unre

vealing.

c) Moon'

s pale-skied
after-sens

ed appear
ance

s.

d) Rosemarie

when your
eyes soft

ly fading in
to my self–

reflecting
touched–sen

sibilitie
s.

e) Light-

sensed cloud
s transpar

ently awaken
ing sun–lit

vista
s.

f) Weeping

willow dried–
down its win

tering time
ly disclos

ures.

g) Some root

s spanning
the dark

ground's in
visible depth

Others lay o
pen-aired

bared of
their nourish

ing source.

h) Mid-December'

s dark-time'
s candle's

persistent
glow.

i) Still no

snow Christ
mas bared of

its light-e
asing contem

plative si
lence

s.

j) Why in

winter do
pine tree

s stop grow
ing their o

vershadow
ings.

k) Birches

in winter
seem ever-the-

more bright
ly intuned.

l) How easy

to compose
apparent

ly profound
treatise

s on 2nd or
3rd rate art

istically
preten

cious en
deavor

s.

a) He knew

the time
would come

(it must
as it does)

as a street
however care

fully paved
yet sudden

ly dead-end
ed.

b) Why then

why now as
mysterious

as time it
self samed

to that al
ways present

ly-here.

c) His life

had been too
good for him

undeserved
yet fully ap

preciat
ed.

136

d) Parent

s who rare
ly under

stood his
why or where

fore yet to
tally devot

ed with a
self-satisfy

ing urge to
their only

son the
youngest.

e) A child

hood fully
protected

not even
under-lipp

ed whisper
ings of that

Jew-time o
ver the for

bidden o
cean.

f) The "dark

years" a de
cade of un

mirrored
fearful

ly-intensed
self-recognit

ion.

g) The scholar

ly papered
and facts of

a people and
time totally

unrelated
to his own.

h) A God dis

tantly call
ing from with

in the cellar
ed darkness

of his own
time-reach.

i) A wife

who brighten
ed his e

very-moment
to a self-o

vercoming
newly-sensed

identity-
cause.

j) A calling

over that
darkly-blood

ed ocean to
voice The Lord

's claims on
a satanical

ly enslaved
people

k) and a

voice once a
gain over

heard fom
its indwell

ing servit
ude

l) pulsed

with renew
ing life

for these
times and o

vertime
s.

a) If poetry'

s as for Portu
gal "a certain

ed identity"
and we read

little of it
now lost in a

wilderness
of no-find

ings-out
where.

b) Do we quest

ion life or
is life it

self daily
dialoguing

us into a
density of

but uncertain
tentative an

swering
s.

c) Constable

felt those
familiar

clouds e
volving his

own painter
ly premonit

ions.

d) Time pass

es through
us as wave

s evoking
continu

ous self-dis
tancing

s.

e) Each self-

chosen friend
stands at-the-

other-side
of our self-

shadowing
interval

s.

f) Those Asch

bachian hill
s descend

ing immanent
ly intelling

time-phrasing
s.

g) And if

Haydn (presum
ably dead) had

really conduct
ed his own

Cherubini
Requiem Mass.

h) Or did

Napoleon
crown himself

to France'
s last-time

blood–ensu
ing great

ness.

i) Dead-pre

suming nation
s today a

rising from
the sea as

Aphrodite
nakedly

self–entic
ing.

j) That high

ly sourced
mountain

took the
shadowing

bottom out
of his dead–

ended precept
ions.

k) Volcanic

islands depth–
emerging

from a sea
of convuls

ing up–surg
ings.

l) Some are

born into
the light of

a nakedly
feared life-

trauma wombed
from the dark

nesses of
their self-

surround
ing reassur

ances.

m) And those

mothers "blue
d" at the

urge of
life's com

pelling birth-
source.

n) Wonder

ing at those
flaming star

s distanc
ing the hea

ven's untell
ing immensit

ies.

144

a) Prime time

empty wait
ing room

filled with
childful

animal-pict
ures the plea

sing middle-
aged doctor

waiting (per
haps for week

s or even
months on end)

for the usual
nothing to

happen.

b) Almost

daily test
s blood-find

ings or scann
ing his secret

ly secluding
interior be

ing's unknown
elusively

hide-out
s.

c) Hide and

seek land
scaping the

untouched
loneliness

of nothing
to be found

out.

d) Waiting

days–on–end
for an an

swer (a
letter or

phone–call)
his timeless

ly uncertain
ed future.

e) As a child

touching the
cool envelop

ing sheets
of the moon'

s self–reveal
ing light–

phrasing
s

f) or the shad

owing of leave
s falling

through his
dream-sensed

time–continu
ities.

g) Fish aquar

iumed their
glass-enclos

ing reflect
ions.

h) Age 11

at left-field
waiting (if

only then)
through

space-confin
ing intensit

ies.

i) Listening

to these poem
s (as now)

for your un
seen time-re

calling pre
ception

s.

j) Ferris-

wheel at the
height of

heavenly
star-preclud

ing distanc
ings.

a) At the a

dolescent
cross-way

s (age 15
or so) Dylan

Thomas' self-en
thusing voiced-

imaging time-
coloring

s

b) or T. S.

Eliot's mind-
set Christ

ianed paper-
paged poet

ics.

c) More likely

Robert Frost'
s tradition

al common-
sensed provin

cial–stead
fastness.

d) And the

oncoming Jaffin
refuged in his

self–reflect
ive word–clean

sing imagin
ings.

a) Does Hist

ory as every
art become

only what it
"really was"

until the af
ter-said real

izes it anew
often other

wise than
its personal

intent?

b) If the winn

ers conceive
"what real

ly happened"
in the image

of their own
success then

the losers
left only

(as the Ameri
can South)

with poetic
untimely re

verie
s.

c) History

as art only
is what it

(in time)
becomes

through its
visual appear

ance as if
the unspoken

wasn't al
ways overhear

ing behind-
the-scene

s.

d) And when

Bach (for ex
ample) Glen

Gould's us
into totally

unassuming
vistas does

the creator
himself lose

his final say
in that creat

ion-of-his-
own.

e) Mendelssohn'

s E Minor Quartet
momentarily

lost (for him)
its especial

ly reflective
transparen

cies when the
Sibelius left

it shadowing
in darkly color

ed pre-concept
ions.

f) Can my momen

tary recept
ivity really

re-fashion
a work-of-

art to the
taste of its

(my) only-
now.

g) (or can)

a work-of–
art's self–

exposure
s reveal e

ven its cer
tained intent

in a newly
transform

ing light

h) (does then)

Ranke's "what
it really is"

refashion
itself in the

guise of Shakes
peare's myster

iously tenta
tive appearan

ces.

i) Does art

(then) pre
sume more than

"the real"
itself.

j) When yester

day become
s the today

of tomorrow'
s pre-assum

ing awareness
es.

k) Staph'

s Kafka be
came just-as–

much his own
as Brod's

though secular
ized to his

alternate
intent.

a) To discover

Pessoa is to
realize more

than the sun'
s depthed–hori

zoning self.

b) Pessoa say

s more than im
plying what

hasn't been
said at all.

c) Pessoa

poems me
back into

those vast
ly undiscov

ered region
s of self.

d) Pessoa'

s night–can
dles where

even the sun'
s thirsting

for light.

Bare-ground

winter only
the sky seem

s to vary
its open–face

intent.

a) When tradit

ion lives–on
as here with

the Christmas
tree's ever–

greenly evocat
ive–familiar

response the
gift–exchang

ing multiple–
children'

s smiles while
the real source

of a truly sus
taining joy

Christ–Himself
lies almost

nakedly–forgott
en buried some

where in a
long–forgott

en past.

b) But now

more–even–
more the bro

ken or self–
assuming "fam

ily's" loneli
ness at–heart.

c) Do they

still hear
that vaguely-

reminiscent
music of its

truly tradit
ional source

d) or does

the money-
business

of exchange
able value

s increase
their with

holding long
for more

of what has
become a senti

mentally van
ishing past

e) (yet)

how surpris
ed young

children'
s eyes seem

to attune
to the Christ

mas tree'
s light–se

ductive source

f) and how

some "ancient"
medieval song

as "We Three
Kings" evoke a

time–telling
longing for

the real just
and loving

king

g) or those

listening
to the essen

tial message
of "God

Bless Ye Merry
Gentlemen"

assuaging
those sensual

even only
dream–evok

ing side-
paths.

h) Even those

church-going
once-a-year

Christian
s rarely

learn of that
circuitous

route from
star-invoking

Bethleham
to its blood–

sacrificial
Golgotha'

s dead–end
ed timeless

victory.

i) How "O Come

All Ye Faithful"
that multi-nat

ional credo-
hymn gather

s the lasting
remnants of

a time-tell
ing past to

newly realiz
ing future

hopes.

j) Have tradit

ions (then)
somehow kept

remotely a
live the real

source of the
genuine light

and peace of
Christmas'

eternal-bless
ings.

a) The poet'

s not a pro
phet (as

Pushkin
would have it)

Dark force
s as those

sudden storm
s at sea

arisen from
the self-de

vouring depth
s of his gen

ius drive him
(as Tolstoy)

from the lov
ing source

of his so–
much–needing

self–bearing
s.

b) The poet'

s not a pro
phet (perhap

s a demonic
one as Lermon

tov would
have it) im

pairing the
very–source

of his much–
needed self–

balancing
judgment.

c) The true

artist's oft
poised at the

fear–consum
ing height

s of his own
self–destruct

ive instinct
ual fall.

d) Art may

realize that
other–side–

of–self but
it must be

tamed as a
wild night–

prowling
creature.

e) The prophet

may (also)
be voiced in

those darken
ing realm

s of The
Lord's impend

ing judgment.

f) He may have

to relinguish
(as Hosea or

Beethoven)
the normative

claims of a
self–satisfy

ing family
life

g) Lord balan

ce me at the
precipice

of those far–
searching

horizon
s but hold

me tight–and–
fast for fear

of falling
into those

self-abandon
ing darken

ing depth
s.

a) Pre-Christ

mas flower
ings off-sea

son (as Christ
will always re

main) yet ever–
so hesitant

ly self-reveal
ing.

b) When patien

ce and prayer
season our off-

balancing
self-defying

premonition
s.

c) The seldom-

momentary
touch of those

love-held
Christ pre-

suming near
nesses.

d) Given-too-

much as David
the prophet-

king may de
mand all-the-

more of a
soul-quench

ing thirst.

e) The true

artist often
remains God'

s-away from
his self-sat

isfying devour
ing claim

s.

f) Rosemarie

helps me to
down-tone

low-tide our
self-sustain

ing love for
"we are less

than this".

Pushkin

(as Schumann)

oft too
youthfully

passionate
ly conceiv

ed to still-
me-down to

those silent
ly time-re

claiming
depth

s.

Zhukowsky'

s "Night"
ed me to the

stilled quiet
udes of my

childhood'
s time-embra

cing dream
s.

When these

off-timed
whitely en

compassing
houses no

longer dress
ed in their

ghostly-es
tranged appear

ances.

a) Why can some

poems become
re-discover

ed in anoth
er language

(as if writt
en for a

multiple
cause)

whereas
dead-to-word

s in yet a
nother.

b) (or why do

some friend
ships cross

that bridged–
together

ness where
as others re

main ultimate
ly time–strand

ed.

c) A poet may

become (will
ingly or not)

a "prophet"
as in the

Russia of en
forced silen

ces where
as in other–

lands other–
times his

voice remain
s uncaged as

a strange
ly–colored pre–

enchanted
bird.

d) Suffering

may source
the interior

confines of
"true art"

whereas a
Bach a Shakes

peare a Haydn
seemingly

not–other
wise–samed

as you–or–
I.

e) Some may

conceive of
distant plan

ets as yet
undiscover

ed landing
surface

s whereas
others be

come fantas
ied to their

strangely-
distant night–

lost dreamed-
reverie

s.

f) Love or in

fatuation
of a woman

hidden in
one's own

(as yet)
evasive

time-scheme
s.

g) Why has

that (so
familiar) o

ther-side-of–
the-room be

come my fa
ther's distant

ly evoking
death–spell.

h) Call it

"chemistry"
but not e

ven George'
s best-equipp

ed laborat
ory could de

cipher that
once-in-a

lifetime
love-virus.

i) Is faith

God's will
pre-ordain

ed for some
(and yet) re

motely undis
covered terr

ain for o
thers.

j) Man may

have been crea

ted equal in
The Lord's un

fathomable
designs but

for most-of–
us he (or

she) remain
s an unequall

ed there-a
bout–

s.

k) Why do some

need sentiment
tal Hollywood

films or
flimsy music

to evoke
(at times)

a genuine re
sponse.

l) Why did

Christ chose
mostly "sim

ple people"
(as fishermen)

for his most-
exclusive

home-catch.

m) Our planet

revolves a
bout an ever-

changing
time-scheme

while we can'
t decipher

the true-
cause of but

a single-
moment.

Baratynsky

It was

your mind
that need

be tempered
(lately

found) a
unity of form

ed-sense.

Christmas-Eve Idyllic *(10)*

a) A generation

of pre-adoles
cent girl

s half-dress
ed in the per

fumed fantasie
s of Barbie-

doll imitative
self-emulat

ions.

b) Such a sweet

prettiness
of artificial

ly scented flow
ering picture-

postcard come-
on girl

s.

c) The once-a-

year Christmas
Eve church-do

ing candle-
lighting their

made-up fully
articulat

ing dress-down
appearance

s.

d) Cherubic

voices in
tuning those

old-time half-
forgotten

Christmas
hymn

s.

e) Such a dis

play of all
those decorat

ive Christmas
trimming

s But where'
s the Christ-

child somehow
lost in a

sea of famil
iar small-town

dignitarie
s.

f) Silent

Night's
tear-clutch

ing old fra
gilely wrought

ladie's once-
upon-a-time'

s sentiment
al recollect

ions.

g) I more-than-

sensed–him–far–
off–to–the–

right stately–e
rect song-book

and prayer'
s full-voiced

readily glow
ing peace-time

adulation
s.

h) The more-

than–middle–
aged dignifi

ed pastor
took right–

up to the
chancel a

highly Christ
ianed book

of less–quot
ed (though
still Christ–

saving) certi
fied example

s.

i) A baby

cried so
sweetly Christ-

like that a
few middle-

aged ladie
s slightly

turned their
half-accentu

ated smile
s.

j) The church

left with rare
ly warm-seat

ed benches
the after-

glow of a
once-upon-a-

time fully-e
quipped parish

for their
daily down-to-

earth money-
making vent

ures.

If Bach Haydn

Mozart and Beet
hoven ... didn'

t know any bett
er than to

write for the
tonal qualitie

s of individual
instrument

s Solists with
a limited re

pertoire help–
them-out by

transscrib
ing it better–

made for
their own self–

satisfying
virtuose-ap

peals.

Ivan Krylov

>a home-spun
>Russian poet
>
>Aesopped-me-
>back to the
>
>everyday
>moral message
>
>s of univer
>sally relevant
>
>truth
>s.

When a poem'

>s too-little-
>fleshed to
>
>realize its
>life-expansive
>
>blood-reign
>s.

A society

>too afraid
>to call-by-
>
>what's e
>vidently self-
>
>apparent.

a) Cloud stud

ies as Consta
ble's mood–

vanishing
thought

s.

b) When the

late autumn
al winds left

behind but
bared-tree'

s remote shad
owing.

c) First love'

s tentative
ly evoking

untouched
silence

s within.

d) Tiny winter

birds feeding
on the last

ing remnant
s of this

ground–aband
oning immin

ent design
s.

e) Why cling

to the wisdom
of ancient

sagas when
the moon's

eclipsed in
transcend

ing darkness
es.

f) When the

stream's sun–
shine bared

to its stone–
surfacing

echoing
s.

g) At the

sea's depth
ed bottom

ness strange
creature

s eying-out
their self-eman

ating light-
shine

s.

h) Turning-

the-corner
into those

self-withhold
ing side-street

s lone-
time appear

ance
s.

i) Why do

those so im
personally

tall Manhatt
an building

s shadow
such isolat

ing time-ex
posure

s.

j) She but mo

mentarily
caught-up

to her mood–
enlighten

ing appear
ance

s.

k) Raphael

sang him

self into a
self-realiz

ing there
ness.

l) That inopport

une lion lei
sured the in

tending warm
th of pleas

urable sun–
length expos

ures.

m) His blue-

checker
ed pajama

s somehow
stimulating

night-time
poetic imag

ining
s.

a) First snow

holding tight
to the branch

ed nakedness
of death'

s persistent
calling

s.

b) This land'

s white-encom

passing grave
enchantment

s.

c) Too bright

now to even
distinguish

the rose'
s last-breath

ed blooming
s.

d) Can one

realize how
time's sub

dued its
raw-earth

ed longing
s.

e) The long-

awaited snow
lighting e

ven the night'
s time-pre

suming dark
nesses.

f) These silent

fields flow
ing the in

creasing dis
tances of their

snow-lit re
verie

s.

Rosemarie

s christmas
tree elegant

ly strung
with the hand-

touched "less
er art" of

momentary
pleasure

able accord
s.

When the

eternal light
of The Lord'

s blessed
holiness

diminish
es into the

expendible
claims of

man's human
ly-sourced

value
s.

a) Pushkin-

Lermontov exil
ed-duelled

into their
blood-arous

ing "prophet
ic" ritual

s.

b) Lermontov'

s darkly demon
ic versed at

perpetual
odds to his

God-seeking
self-consum

ing right
eousness.

a) That snowed-

down feeling
of a self-re

vealing clean
liness.

b) Breughel'

s "Children'
s Games" snow-

delighting
casual time-

appearance
s.

c) These dis

parate poem
s vainly re

cycling time'
s secluding

mysterie
s.

d) Line-branch

ed snow-fin
gering fra

gile rhythm
ic-impulsing

s.

a) December 26th

2nd day of
Christmas

here as if
the first had

n't fully ac
comodated

His timeless
blessing

s.

b) If they'

re no-stop
s-left track

ed to endless
ly snow-re

vealing landscap
ings.

c) Some mother

s too proud
to release

their son'
s womb-impend

ing bondage.

Rosemarie'

s rounding
neck-pearled

to self-sus
taining glad

nesses.

a) Tyutchev

two-direction
ed his soul

ful climb
s as if Ja

cob's ladder
earth-bound

in perpetual
darkness

sensed.

b) His late

love's endang
ered premonit

ions as of
dream's soul

enchanted
death-flow

s increasing
tides.

The rich

tones of Mar
ais' gamba con

sorts swept
through the

darkening
depths of his

mind's time-
recurring

imagining
s.

a) Lost chan

ces may recur
again if

only (even
more) dream-

sourced.

b) Continuity

What we re
member (or

not) become
s colored

by time's
increasing

ly overheard
awareness

es.

c) Those who

would redeem
their unfor

gotten fault
s may discov

er in time
the persisten

cy of that
outlasting

cause.

d) He rowed

through those
unevened wave

s of time'
s reluctant

ly shored-re
membrance

s.

e) The night

snowed itself
into perpet

ually unassum
ing shadow

s.

f) Are birth

and death
pained with

the same o
pen-ended

future.

g) Some con

tinue to re
live moment

s of a vast
ly uncertain

ed past.

h) Why have

those common
ly recurring

places rout
ined us to

their dulled
sense of un

timely unex
pectant fore

boding
s.

i) Those dark

ly intuned
birds left

the freshly-
fallen snow

with but mo
mentarily-se

cured im
pression

s.

j) Rosemarie

let us time
ly-forget

each day
lives us but

one-step clo
ser to an un

certained-
future.

k) These

clouds time-
shifting per

spective
s shadow

ing a ten
tatively

self-invok
ing cause.

l) Why speak

of vain hope
s when Miss

Blackburn'
s 2nd grade

blackboard
daily eras

ing a time-
cleansing

fitness.

a) Alexei Tolstoy

as Donne
poet of love

and of love
formed at

its eternal
source time

lessly true.

b) The distan

cing time-se
quence of Fet'

s verse as
my 2nd read

unevened
mood–sens

ing.

c) Late romant

ic here as
there press

ed-out as a
plump but

sapless o
range juic

ed.

d) Ivan Bunin

somehow a
part on the

surface
of a light

ly depthed
mood-conscious

ness.

a) Her father

a behind-the-
back kind-of-

personed a
daughter in

his own schem
ing image.

b) They under

stood each o
ther's friend

ly façade
s all–too–

well to hide
from those

self–conceal
ing persuas

ions.

c) Was she

evil or was
she sick

at the pois
oned root

of her very
being.

d) She lived-

it–out never

theless afraid
of her own

self–transform
ing identity.

e) until one

preconceiv
ed day she

mirrored
her true self

sourced in
to the bleak

depth of a
bottomless

emptiness.

a) Night-time

snow awaken
ing shadow

s of an ir
reconcil

able past.

b) Fields

of snow dis
tancing the

length of
time's immen

sing future.

c) Car light

s in the
night's a

waring
through its

snow-drift
ing past.

d) When the

continu
ously sensed

snowed an unre
solving same

ness.

e) Silent

streets e
vening-out

rediscover
ing time-

length
s.

f) When a

darkly invis
ible bird

left behind
its shadow

lessly self-es
caping iden

tity.

g) Why she

feared most–
of–all the

night of her
own secret

ly interior
design

s.

h) That time-

transcend
ing moon wit

nessing
worlds of

self-invok
ing silenc

es.

i) It night

ly evolved
from the yes

terday of the
day's dream–

escaping
time-wave

s.

a) He often

preferred
beautified wo

men's facially-
stoned untouch

able shadow
ings.

b) It was

only when he
imaged his

thought-touch
ed imagining

s that poem
took-on its

securely with
holding self–

resolve.

c) Not what'

s said but
those momen

tarily sens
ed wind-phras

ings.

d) Mendelssohn'

s scherzi
freshly bree

zed light-sur
facing

s.

e) Oft over-

stated as
Beethoven'

s dramatic-
acclaim

s there still
remains more

untouchable
silences in

the star'
s light-awak

ening
s.

f) The purity

of the musical
ly line-depth

ed transpar
encies of the

great Renaiss
ance master

s.

g) Snowed-in

to a surround
ing sense of

self-enclos
ing still

nesses.

h) This night-

snow's darkly
encompass

ing wind-ensu
ing bright

nesses.

Once again

a Malaysian
plane lost

somewhere
in the ocean'

s self-inhab
iting darken

ings.

Alexander

Blok tension
ed and seduc

ed by the
night-wine'

s self-decept
ive lustful

urging
s.

An open

door to the
room's empti

ness-calling
s.

Our family

shipped to a
self-securing

hold but fly
ing under

strangely re
mote flags two–

samed that final
port's signify

ing light
s.

"First the

Jews then the
Christian

s" a motto
we've heard be

fore now echo
ing through

those ancient
lands of their

faith-wombed
origin

s.

a) The less

one knows (e
ven of one

self) the
better it is

We all lead
a curtain

ed existence
darkly self–

shadowing.

b) Now I under

stand those
glass–confin

ed closed–
off book shelv

es' scarcely
decipher

able title
s hidden for

years from un
touchable re

membranc
es.

c) My father

though a law

yer of pene
trating quest

ions still liv
ed a fairy-tale-

kind-of-life
behind a fa

çade of un
touchable

myths.

d) Their cost

ly Persian
carpet remain

ed (even after
years of

only visible
appearance)

distinctly
kept from un

finely use.

e) She may

have kept her
old clothes

closeted a
way but now-

and-then (oft
at odd-hour

s) she open
ed the door

to their in
extinguish

able past.

f) Why did

those once-
time love-lett

ers from an
unfaithful

suitor still
remain neat

ly sorted in
the attic

staired-away
from view.

g) Old demense

persons inhab
iting a lone

ly sensed
room of memor

able silenc
es.

h) Some new

ly-found Christ
ians still re

main delight
fully impress

ioned by the
tragic fate

of once close
ly-felt class

mates.

i) She often

woke-up to
the dark of

moon-lit
self-witness

ing fear
s.

j) "The whole

truth and
nothing but

the truth"
emptied him

nakedly–down
see–levell

ed.

k) She need

ed those
little fine

ly–kept bric–
à–brac to

touch back
her once–in

tact child
hood rever

ies.

l) My brother-

in-law though
vividly criti

cal of one-
and-all still

kept to his
repeatedly

democratic
ally-intuned

Whitmanes
que self-a

vowels.

m) That short-

distance
view across

a self-enclos
ing lake

still opened
for him a

widely-sens
ed breadth of

poetic-intuit
ions.

a) It snow

ed his time-
securing

sense-of-
self away in

to current
s of dream-

evoking shad
owless con

templation
s.

b) The continu

ous snow'
s wind-shift

ing light-
field

s.

c) "White-on

white" remain
ed convass

ed to a stat
ic self-suffi

ciency.

d) Snow-fanta

sied night e
merging

through the
mind's increas

ing aware
ness.

e) The yester

day of tomorr
ow's vastly

snowed–light
sameness

es.

f) The wood'

s darkly con
cealing now

mysterious
ly brighten

ing an expan
se of light–

purifying
conscious

ness.

g) Nightly-

sensed animal

tracks in
snow left but

a blood-
tentative

impression
of somewhere

s-else-from-
now.
h) When the

snow finally
stopped a

breathless
ly untouch

able silence.

i) Snow-dream

s awakening

light-sens
ing time-trans

parencie
s.

j) Can the

once still–
foreboding

night now
snow–light

fantasied.

k) No human

art (not e
ven Monet'

s evanescent
impression

ism) can imi
tate the

phantomed
realms of

snow's light–
overcoming

timeless
ness.

l) Snow wind

s the innuen
does of

Rosemarie'
s love–dream

ed eye
s.

m) Even far-

out–at–sea
those winter

ed ships wav
ed–through

time-snowed
remembran

ces.

a) Tsvetaeva

a poetess
of neither–

here–nor–
there wander

ing an abyss
of rhyme–rhyth

mic other–sens
ings.

b) Pasternak'

s early non–
stop restless

ly versed–
me–out some

where well bey
ond time-con

trol.

c) Pasternak

could rhyme

later (at
times) in beau

tified versed-
stillness

es.

d) His momen

tary there'
s nowhere

s-else-than-
now.

a) This end

less snow im
pression

ed his mind
to a spacious

sense of time
lessness

b) as when

a summerly
blue heaven

s its light–
uplifting

source.

c) Rosemarie

the touch of
your softly

involving
hair feels

me that way
too

d) as when

soothing Flor
idian wave

s voice an
expanse of

self–renew
ing quietude

s.

e) Why need

of paradisi
cal perspect

ives when
Here's the

all of al
ways–more.

f) Victoria'

s "O Magnum
Mysterium"

purifying
the realm

s of spirit
ual identi

ty.

g) The snow

increasing
ly sensed the

reclining
ease of a

voiceless
presence.

h) as when

Wallace Steven'
s "Two Letter

s" the time
less satis

faction of
an always

self-return
ing

i) or the "Re

quiem Aeter
num" of Fauré'

s self-resolv
ing home-

coming.

j) The snow

mildly re
claiming

the soft
curves of

these hill'
s gently ac

cepting in
folding

s.

k) When the

pale moon
mirroring

the pond'
s recept

ive wave-
length

s.

l) or when

nothing need
s-be-

said Just
the-two-of-

us and the
room's time-

familiar
presence.

Brodsky'

s tone his al
most time-tell

ing attitude
didn't take me

down more step
s than I could

have evasive
ly left-be

hind.

Noon-time

branch–envelop
ing winter

ed stillness
es as a moth

er coolly reti
cent of her

children'
s remote dis

tancing
s.

Cézanne *(for Lenore)*

repeatedly
satisfie

s the stead
ied posture

s of my time
fully certi

fied well–
being.

a) Who need

s the addition
al even-sens

ed length of
spaceless

ly spelling-
it-all-out

or catalog
ing what-e

ver-for ful
fillment-

sake

b) whereas

justly said'
s all-now

nothing
more.

c) This deep

ly content
ed snow ex

pression
s nothing

more than
its sclf-re

vealing speech
lessness.

Children'

s games their
life-pursu

ing first-
start

s.

a) Time'

s steady rhyme
and rhythm

rarely real
izes our own

unevened
response.

b) The older

we become stead
ing-down with

age the quick
er time e

volves its
own self-con

tinuity.

c) Why the

first time'
s length

seems so
much longer

shadowing
those alway

s increas
ing distanc

es.

d) Only a

shallow-
timed love

continue
s to lose

its own un
certained

persisten
cy.

e) Slower

tempi either
sentimental

ize unsub
stancial

growth-finds
or deepen in

to those soul
ful depth-re

gions.

f) More unre

vealed space
in all the

arts renew
s the inten

sity of one'
s own respon

sive time-
flow.

g) The yester

day of to
day's tomorr

ow's its own
unreveal

ing continu
ity.
h) The after

noon shadow
s our own

seasonal-
response.

i) Quicker

timed person
s often real

ize a great
er depth of

inwardly
self-reveal

ing still
nesses

j) turning-the-

calendar

ed-page to a
papered sense-

of-empti
ness.

k) *Why does*

the melt
ing snow con

tinue to shad
ow our ever–

present time-
sense.

l) *Does the*

river curr
ent our own

change
able rhythm

ic–response.

m) *Her self-*

withhold
ing time-

glance
d him into

those darken
ing self–

shadowing
s.

n) Scars

dale has
past-timed

some of his
most poetic

ally-sensed
reflectiv

ity.

o) Does that

first snow re-

time our own
poetic sensi

bilitie
s.

p) Can time e

rase (as with
Miss Blackburn'

s black board)
some of those

most-attuned
self-certain

ties.

q) Did he

grow into
another per

son or another
timed-being

always-in-
flux.

r) Meaning

ful works-of-
art as Shakes

peare's re
time their

always self-
presence.

s) Sometime

s misplaced
words seem

to haunt his
own self-re

flective
time-sense.

t) That too-

often-said
untimes its

own echoing
resolve.

u) When one

poem lead
s to another

no-ways of
timing their

unfinished-
start.

v) The wave'

s consistent
rhythmic

flowing in
to a time

less contin
uity

w) or those

personal
ly secret en

closure
s to her

slowly in
volving

quietude
s.

x) now

seemingly
lost under the

snow's impend
ing time-

closure
s.

a) Snowed-

doomed morn
ing's awaken

ing to a
blood–Russ

ian indigen
ous–past.

b) My grand

parents got–
out of the

Russian
soul-sensed

blood–fear
ed Jewish

past as the
last German

survivor
s American

ized to that
accumulat

ive freed
om of dollar

s and cent'
s smiling–

ups.

a) "Unbelievab

ly beautiful
women" (as

Allan B.
would put–it)

may believe–
him–out of

his too–pene
trating mouth–

watering
close–up

s.

b) Pink master

ed his subtle
ly self–intun

ing smile
d an appre

ciative "let'
s hear more

from you"
almost lett

ering his
self–decept

ive moment
ary impress

ions.

As if there'

s a continu
ity to the

landscap
ing vastness

of this snow-
appealing

always-seen.

a) This January

snow's time-
brighten

ing its sun-
immensing

light-expans
es.

b) These fresh

ly-watered

primely-sens
ed flower

ing an ever-
ready sun-

shined exist
ence.

c) Your Sun

day smile
d me right

into those
church-bell'

s bright
ly–intuned

light-calling
s.

a) Writing

himself in
to the heart

of winter'
s bleak no–

man's-land'
s never-re

turns.

b) My father

skillfully
denied his 90–

year-old ag
ing as if Ponce

de Leon had dis
covered his age

less youth not
Florida's perenn

ial fountain
s.

c) Can we con

tinually de
lude ourselve

s into
fantasie'

s other-time
s reclusive

ly self-sat
isfying

d) though

those daily
poems clutch

at that same
life-holding

"haven't-
said-it-all"

as the 26-
year-old Keat

s.

e) Those peace-

deluding time-
shadowing

grave-yards
haven't been

calling me by
my youthful

ly-consoling
name yet.

f) And if Rose

marie died-
out the out-

lasting hope
s of these

primely-kept
flowering

delusion
s.

g) The winter'

s self-conceal
ing light

rising from
its sound

lessly time-
lifting birth-

rites.

h) He mirror

himself into
a youthful

aging-at-the-
limbs Adon

is.

i) Once a

fear as a
dart sudden

ly penetrat
ed Pink's soul

ful self-ful
filling life-

timed comfort
s.

j) As the

swing-hold
ing heaven

ly-entranc
ed child-like

dream-rever
ies.

k) And when

the less than
life-long

friends dis
appearing

one-by-one
voiceless

ly other-
timed.

l) As when

spring change
d faces left–

him (not yet)
those winter–

abandoning
light–phas

ings

m) and those

blank irre
trievably

nameless
space

s.

n) "Face-up-

to–the–fact
s" as if my

father hadn'
t always

dreamed–past
those elusive

ly–vacant call
ings.

a) Rediscover

ing Haydn's Bary
ton Trio's sim

plicity (at
times) so in

tricately
even intimate

ly refined.

b) and those

darkly-sensed
irretriev

able color
ings.

"Japonaise" *(Folkwang Museum, Essen) (7)*

    a) Redon'

s flowers

color-discover
ing an inten

sity of light-
awareness

es.

b) *Gauguin's*

Riders on the
Beach's irre

trievably
lightness

of time-re
sponsive im

pression
s.

c) *At its*

best the fra
gile poetic

sensibility
of Japanese

art too fine
for the immi

tative refine
ments of Europ

ean taste.

d) *Waves of sus*

pending color
ed depth-en

closure
s.

e) Birds more

the light and
air of wingèd

transparen
cies.

f) A foliage

of almost un
touchably-

sensed refine
ments.

g) Rain awak

ens unsuspect
ing darkness-

enclosure
s.

Plane-time *(Personae) (11)*

a) Her prominent

ly fixed-teeth
artificial

ly open-mouth
ed a perfum

ed lip-stick
smile.

b) Plane'

s space-glid
ing left it

relative
ly out-side

his perpetua
ting cold-

front posture
s.

c) Almost angel

ically she
warmed an effus

ively cloud-
surrounding

aura.

d) Good-enough

for T. V.'s
low-profiled

"I've-seen-
it-all-be

fore" imitat
ions.

e) Near-death

experienc
ed her accid

ent-prone
too easily

hurt-through
sensibiliti

ies.

f) The upgrading

sensuality
of his close

ly-viewed
most intim

ately-respons
ive exposure

s.

g) He eye-ball

ed bare-skull
ed toothless

ly self-imman
ently smil

ing.

h) Winding

stair-cased
his uphold

ing virtuoso
attuned

Pink-like
smile-length

s.

i) His Florid

ian beach-
length self-

attuning imit
ative well

nesses.

j) That con

stant narrow–
pathed him to

a straight–
line uphold

ing self-re
assurance.

k) R. B.

Was she the
one who i

maged-him–
back to a re

birthed sense
of receptive

time-being.

a) Is U. S.

T. V. violence
perpetual

ly committ
ed to a pre–

assuming state
of that al

ways-being
now

b) and or

is it in
turn the creat

or of what
it's alway

s set–out
as its own

self–becoming.

Poems from Florida *(13)*

a) Floridian

cloud–swell

s one into
a discontin

uity of warm
th time–ris

ers.

b) This Florid

ian night as
if fathomed

into the
depth of these

starless
space–evok

ing wind
s.

c) Dark wave

soundless
ly surfac

ing the hori
zons of the

mind's time
less reach.

d) This all-pre

vading still
ness as if e

ven those un
spoken word

s echoing
their breath–

withhold
ing resolve.

d) When not e

ven touch re
leases the un

touchable
realms of

this forebod
ing darkness.

e) If it was

all origined
here out of

the darkness
of The Lord'

s time-reclaim
ing word.

f) The wing

èd pelican'
s wind–eas

ing quiet
udes.

g) Palms

reaching-out
their space

less soul-
searching

s.

h) Invisible

tropical
winds breath

lessly time-
enchanting.

i) Not even the

artificial
ly speechless

high-rises
can diminish

this secret
ly-sensed Ind

ian past.

j) This metall

ic railing
touching

through the
coolness

of its light-
withholding

static-de
sign.

k) Where

these swamped–
grasses loom

ing with the
snake's venu

mous glow.

l) Can one

tame the prim
itive urging

s of night'
s instinct

ual desire
s.

a) Floridian

sun-rise hori
zoned to the

sand–length
distancing

s of sound
less imagin

ings.

b) Surfacing

this flat–
down beaches'

wind–phrasing
impression

s.

For Daryl *(3)*

a) The sermon

no-other-way-
than mine dir

ectioned pre
cisely at

the heart's
inevitable

cause.

b) To deny

that truth
as if person

ed in an a
lien ident

ity.

c) The Lord

rebirths at
the source

of its blood–
renewing

claims.

Floridian

beach–Sunday
s heighten

ed to the
time-coloring

of umbrellar
ed–assuming

gladness
es.

The waning

flags of late
afternoon

shadowing
the fading

hopes of Amer
ica's eclips

ing imperial-
design

s.

Eerie

> ghost-like
> fog-encom
>
> passing sha
> dowless si
>
> lence
> s.

To judge

> a work-of-
> art only on
>
> its interior
> merits ups
>
> Leibl's levell
> ing-at Cour
>
> bet.

The need

> to kiss Rose
> marie to the
>
> depth of a
> lasting
>
> strength.

Night

ship at sea
darkening

into its
indecipher

able cause.

a) She left

me with the
impression

of a shadow
less self-supp

orting tree.

b) She order

ed her make-
shift self pre

sentably
time-present.

c) Why ask of

a shadowless
Chinese land

scape mirror
ing your own

wordless
ly intact

self.

a) Snap-shot

s shooting
that fleet

ingly color
ed bird as

Goya's "pluck
ed feather's"

dead–down.

b) That pre-

destined nation
renamed only

after Columbus'
mapped–down

pursuit
s.

c) Why imagine

poetic sensi
bilities imag

ed to but a
single depth-

scented rose.

d) He hurried

his late-after
noon shadow

ing steps
past their

pre-attend
ing mark.

e) St. Peter

may also have
briefly walked-

on-waves but
only for a

momentary
self-shadow

ing.

f) The "Holy

Christian
Church" may

have blood-
drawn its Jew

ish master
at the cost

of protect
ing its down-

ridden soul.

g) Movies may

scenically
poetize what

the stage
leaves bared-

down Strind
bergian empt

ied-faced.

h) "Writing-

it-off" those
blood-instinct

ual temptat
ions.

i) He sat in

church front–
rowed but his

sensed–aware
nesses remain

ed back–row
ed down–town

ed.

a) Sunrise

across the
Gulf's light–

imbuing horiz
oned still

nesses.

b) The supple

thin–length
ed palm's

softly in
volving breeze–

flow.

c) Riding

the beaches'
flat-down

wind-sensed
time-expanse

s.

d) Have these

distant wave
s been mess

aged to re
birth contin

uing silence
s.

e) The wide-ex

panses of The
Gulf's cloud-

immersing
transparen

cies.

f) Shell-touch

ed fingered-
impelling fra

gile time-re
currence

s.

g) The warmth

slow-down of
these spacious

ly self-reass
uring time-en

closing attune
ments.

h) Those dis

tances farther

always-farther
than our color-

sustaining
light-need

s.

a) A poem

however time-
satisfying

elusive
ly soul-sens

ed.

b) Form only

completes it
self when you

(and no-one-
else) real

izes its al
ways-so.

c) The Living

God continue
s to witness

His light-trans
scending dark

nesses.

d) The ocean

transparent
ly depthed

in time-sus
pending clari

ties.

e) He hesitant

ly awaited
(if only mo

mentarily)
space-secur

ing certaint
ies.

f) Why dream

of obscured
and exotic

lands when
each-of-our-

steps still
remains time-

escaping.

g) Distant

ly skied-
birds reveal

ing even more
than our own

spacious-i
magining

s.

h) Aquarium-

fish only arti
ficially

glass-reflect
ing?

i) Even short

distance
s can shadow

our time-
tensed self-

sufficien
ces.

j) Do land-

locked–salmon
or winter–a

bandoned
birds real

ize a need
for escaping

time–hold
s.

k) When that

self–sustain
ing room be

came his
only world

of timed–
remembran

ces.

l) Van Gogh'

s time–immens
ing sun–shad

owing the sow
er's self–re

flecting si
lence

s.

m) When his

poetry become
s an all-in

clusive world
of self-satis

fying an al
ways only–

there.

n) Even these

night-intens
ing artifi

cial light
s personal

ly voiced.

Shakespearian (5)

a) I'm so

glad my mother
wasn't one of

those who in
sisted as Lady

Macbeth a re
peated hand-wash

ing for the
sake of daily

cleanliness.

b) Hamlet

stage-fright
behind-the-

curtain for
repeated self-

shadowing
s.

c) Barney

my grandfath
er role-modell

ed King Lear
for his child

ren's respect
ful upbring

ing.

d) As an ex

ample of posit
ive thinking

she readily
espoused Lady

Macbeth's con
sistency as

action-in-pur
pose.

e) Let's con

tinually learn
from Othello'

s always-on–
the-alert o

pen-eared for
suspicious

behavior.

Shylock

all eyes and
ears for the

weight of
traditional

value
s.

a) The ocean'

s soundless
depthed un

resolving
darkness

es.

b) Inland

waterway
's the se

clusive realm
of indigen

ous bird-
coloring

s.

c) "Genuine

Floridians"
a rare spec

ies here oft
racially

self-exclu
sive.

d) If one

listens hard
enough the

low-down
breath-sens

ing Indian
thunder-in

stinct
s.

e) These

sands paled
into sur

facing dis
tance

s.

a) Time-shar

ing while

space-shar
ing a taste

of what isn'
t ours alone

for that
roomed-in

privacy.

b) Daily a

mirroring-
back of

our chang
ing time

less selve
s.

c) Living the

intimacie
s of a 2nd

marriage
housed in her

husband'
s first wife'

s taste-de
fines.

d) After a

year-of-ab
sence levell

ing friend
ships back

to a contin
uing perspect

ive-source.

e) Does a

newly repaint
ed house change

one's own
sense of new

ly refresh
ing comfort

s.

f) If "until

death parts
us" the still

continuing
persistent

remembran
ce of past

time's inti
macie

s.

g) 2nd start

as if we
could become

remodelled
to an other

wise sense-
of-self.

h) For-the-

sake-of-com
panionship

afloat again
in foreign

waters?

i) *"I'm alway*

s true to you
darling in

my fashion"
These inti

mately pro
vocative

ly sensed-
feeling

s.

j) *Leverate*

Marriage

if we'll
meet again

which wife
which time

lessly es
poused pre

sent.

k) If "happy

marriages are
made in heav

en" why earth-
them-out a

gain down-
here in our

own self-con
ceiving i

mage.

l) "Live-life"

they say not
the death of

a lifeless
ly present

past-time.

When the

ink runs-out
blood-dried

death of a
timeless

muse.

Pelican

    s gliding
    the height

    of an immea
    surable ease.

Quick-answer

    s at time
    s as fast as

    the dart's
    swiftly pene

    trating blood–
    wound

    s.

Palm

    leaves sway
    ing their

    light-cool
    ing phrase

    s.

a) Horse-shoe

s metallic
ally resound

ing their
surfacing

intention
s.

b) The self-in

creasing aes
thetic of

golf ball'
s distanc

ing time-
span.

c) The fisher

man's invis
ibly depthed

expectat
ions.

d) Shuffle-

board's lin
ear confin

ing evened
eye-control.

e) The eternal

swimmer outlast
ing the water'

s receding
persuasion

s.

a) Distant

buildings
looming bey

ond the mind'
s stone-sens

ed imagining
s.

b) Gauguin'

s "Blue Tree
s" abstract

ing the elus
ive design

s of meta
physical

landscap
ed perspect

ives.

a) Cold wind

s from the
north compell

ing abstract
star-distan

cings.

b) The moon

now plastical
ly self-defin

ing stone-in
tense.

c) Even Linda

Gluckman'
s severe

words once-
again cutt

ing-through
time's vague

ly receptive
remembran

ces.

d) Chinese

shadowless
landscap

ing impli
citly re

mote.

e) The feel

of stone'
s cool-in

spoken aware
nesses.

f) That past-

image stead
ily advanc

ing closer-
to-mind.

g) Haydn'

s piano son
ata's echo

lessly time-
impacting.

h) Late Cour

bet's wave-
rock struct

ured inten
sitie

s.

i) That cold

impenetrat
ing demand

of "The
truth the

whole truth
nothing but

the truth".

j) When water

colors pale
of their o

therwise
time-hold

ing intent.

k) Even Hölderlin'

s rhetorical
higher-ground'

s steadfast
ly self-re

assuring.

l) Poussin

impacting
the landscape'

s classical
firmness.

m) The war-

time dead
stoned to

rows of anony
mous time

lessness.

n) High-rise

s beyond their
shadowless

light–witness
ings.

o) Glück

columned
to the height

ened scope
of classical

abstract
ion.

p) Beethoven

in c minor
leaves me

rushing for
the protect

ive high-
ground of a

Waldstein-
like time-se

curing hold.

a) Aunt Sylvia

denying what
ever womanly

softness
could tame

her harden
ed desire

s for wealth
power and

increased
social influ

ence.

b) Her daught

er Sandra as
head-strong

ambitous
as her mother'

s go-get-'em
s no-holds-

barred.

c) Her husband

Uncle Morton
an Esau-of-a-

man brawned
bodily hair

ed wild-game
dentist.

d) Madeline

that other
wise off-

shoot delicate
ly feminine

sensitive
ly cherish

ing her home-
timed unfulfill

ed longings –
cancer-dead

at 31.

a) Low-tide

bare-beach
ed poem's

birthed-ori
gins.

b) The low

tides of ex
pansive

light-awaken
ings.

c) When the

waves have
calmed their

incessant
tidal-urging

s.

Basho (Haiku) (4)

a) What the

words imply

must settle-
down paper

ing's intent.

b) Only the

fullness
of sound'

s time-re
vealing.

c) Where the

winds have
blown his

transient
thoughts

far–timed.

d) Only an i

mage aspiring
more of its

mood's evan
escent–long

ings.

Old stamp

s and coin
s oft leave

me far–time
sensing.

Even her

hair weight
ed–down to

a time–spend
ing heavi

ness.

After the Japanese (23)

a) Even the

birds left be
hind invis

ible time–
shadowing

s.

b) When leave

s green un
touchable

wind–trans
parencie

s.

c) A bridge

timeless
ly light-in

tent.

d) Waves

depth-immens
ing.

e) The lasting

image of his
mind's increa

singly pre
sent.

f) Poem'

s wordless
ly present.

g) Why need

of more than
clouds evan

escently
wind-send

ing.

h) The upright

tree straight-
lined him ten

tative-
firmly.

i) Waves sur

facing a
timeless ex

panse.

j) Dream

s time-e
lusive pre

sence.

k) When lone

lines vacant
ly time–spac

ing.

l) Bird'

s wingèd
transpar

ent color
ings.

m) Only the

cloud-spok
en image

voiced.

n) This mo

mentary time
less void.

o) A room

personed
with reapp

earing re
membranc

es.

p) When

touch recede
s into

spaced-i
magin

ings.

q) A fear

shadow
lessly night–

awaken
ing.

r) When our

love merge
s into a

unity of
self-appear

ance
s.

s) Abandon

ed planet'
s stone–

darkened
distanc

ings.

t) The swan'

s self-en
closing

whiteness.

u) Stone'

s transpar
ently touch

ed resonan
ce.

v) When the

night's si
lently lift

ed beyond
its outtell

ing dark
ness-reach.

w) If only

now time
lessly self–

transcend
ing.

x) When Rose

marie smile
s my fear

s into
transient

waves of
morning'

s light-a
wakening

s.

He "went-out-

on-a-limb"

as birds u
sually do

with their
time-weight

ing song
s.

Foot-not

ing poems or
(as with the

Haiku) im
plying a trad

ition little
known to

most out-
poems their

essential-
being.

a) Some

thing off-
balanc

ing her self-
protective

openness

b) and that

look remote
ly touch

ing a side-
angled view

ed-self.

a) Sensed

though not
realized at

first some
thing miss

ing.

b) As the late

autumnal

fields emp
ty-sound

ed.

c) As a

room abandon
ed of your

lifeful pre
sence.

d) As a flow

erless cold

and vacant
spring.

e) As those

Cretian sea
s fished–

out of all
their color

ed awareness
es.

f) As those

medieval
side-street

s mysterious
ly past-tim

ed.

g) As when

your mind
runs vacant

h) as a poem

denying its
own self-cer

tainty.

i) As field

s of sunflow
ers now face

lessly clos
ed

j) as those

shadowless
Chinese land

scape
s.

k) As full-

time love
now scarce

ly blossom
ing

l) As a touch

cold to re
membrance.

m) As a boat

stranded on
an emptied

shore.

n) As the lone

liness of a
moonless

night.

o) As a mother
less child.

p) As a ser
mon cold
lifeless
ly abstract.

q) As those
Jewish child
ren night
fully track
ed to strange

and foreign
lands.

r) As time

that has
ceased

to tell.

s) As a butter

fly lost o
ver tide

less water
s.

t) As artifi

cial flower
s dried-down

from touch.

u) As a house

abandoned
to wind and

weather.

v) As the

voiceless
scent of

these prim

ieval wood

s.

w) Yes, where

are those ex
otically-

poised great
blue heron

s — some
thing miss

ing.

As a child

a) *When as*

a child I
could still

feel those
cool sheet

s on a moon
less night.

b) *When as*

a child moth
er prayed me

into a
silently

self-enclos
ing sleep.

c) *When as a*

child autum
nal leave

s falling
through re

flective
silence

s.

d) When as

a child each

step routed
beyond an un

known there
ness.
e) When as a
child that

garden-view
greened in

to poetic a
wareness.

f) When as

a child the
darkness

feared as
an unknown

person.

g) When as a

child The Lord
quietly in

waiting for
time-recording

my praycr
s.

h) Those early

days when I
didn't see

through my
mother's trans

parently still-
holding love-

me.

i) When the

train stopped
mid-night

Albany my
sleepless

ly awake mo
mentary fear

s.

j) The bird

shadowed
ever-closer

his most in
timately fear

ed-presence.

Still the

wind–cold
chill of a

Floridian
paled bright

ness.

No art can

equal the poem'
s all-inclus

ive sense-
sound evocat

ively imagin
ed complete

ness.

Only the

lithe–elusive
designs of a

Japanese
lady can dress

her into
those faint

ly withhold
ing smile

s.

Pelican

s searching
the heaven

s for their
wind-instinct

ual flight.

Saturday

marriage on
the beach as

procession
ally rowed as

gulls attun
ed to their

attentive
ly transform

ing sun-gaz
ings.

Tiny child

ren amassing
swelling sand-

mound's unans
wering call.

a) Dark wave

s timing one'
s own depth

ed-rhythm to
the night's

moonful wit
nessing

s.

b) When with

out warning his
always-timed

heart simply
stopped at

its pre-deter
mining moment.

c) Why ask of

the distant
stars when

this darkness
ever-prevad

ing night's
rhythmic-

flow.

d) The ebb-

and–flow of
a continual

ly repeat
ing heart–

beat.

e) Palm leave

s ceremonious
ly responding

to the wind'
s reassuring

question
s.

f) Spaced-si

lences reach
ing-out to

their preassum
ing distance

s.

a) A 2nd marr

iage can't be
recreated

in the un
timely image

of the first.

b) Why assent

to what's be
come the

wrong-way-
out.

c) The racist

Bilbo at least
met his black

s in the kit
chen of his

back-roomed
person.

d) Are their

alternate
routes left

to finding
one's own e

qualled time-
distance.

e) A woman'

s change-of-
dress (even

the newly ac
quired bright

ly eye-command
ing one) 's

the same e
ven after re

peated mirror
ed-smiling

s.

f) America

"land of the
free and the

brave" re
treating

flags-down
from its own

self-proclaim
ing timeless

certaint
ies.

g) Is masked-

theater more
self-reveal

ing than
Strindberg'

s bared-down
life-stage.

h) For Chung

Ho Chi Minh
national

ist or commun
ist or a u

nity of in
terchange

able time-
current

s.

i) Is self-re

vealing nak

edness only
when she for

got to eye-
brow and lip-

stick her
time–assum

ing feature
s.

j) Why does

the inconstant
moon continue

to wax and
wane when

you're so
certainly

self-defin
ing.

k) A land-

based sailor
still afloat

with tidal re
appearance

s.

l) Their

warmth hand–
holding a de

ceptively
attuning

self-reali
zation?

m) Which to

prefer their
primitive

fear-breed
ing natural

ways or the
veneer of a

Christian
ized pale–

face.

n) However

much she
tried loving

him into
her pre-tim

ed continu
ous affect

ions.

o) When a wo

man has child
rened so much

of her own
blood and

sense than
her husband

could fully
realize his

own claims–
on–her.

p) When friend

s become mere
side–affect

s of an im
pending marit

al crisis.

q) That steel-

down railing
depthed the

time–length
of his firm

ly imprison
ed thought

s.

Darkened identities

a) Those unpre

pared moment
s as when

time sudden
ly overcome

s those care
fully mapped-

out plans-of-
ours.

b) A snake of

unknown ori
gins immovab

ly there
just-read

ied to strike.

c) Jew-blood

dried-down
the earth's

enveloping-
hold.

d) Treasure-

gold tarnish
ing the un

fathomed
depths of the

ocean's secre
tive quietude

s.

e) When her se

ductively
clothed–beauty

ceased to
tempt men'

s flesh–prom
pting eye

s.

f) Changed-

times even
the rediscov

ered language
of poetic–ex

pressive
ness.

g) Hide-and-

seek the blind-
depth of their

still darken
ed identity.

h) When all-

the-clock
s in his

time-consum
ing shop

stopped at
their varied-

interval
s.

i) Aging

men time-in
voking their

irretriev
able child

hood imagin
ings.

j) The Flori

dian morning
slowly dawn

ed the dis
tant horiz

ons of its
time-impell

ing light-a
wareness

es.

k) Love at

the first
sense of her

time-seclud
ing beauty.

l) Animal-

eyes staring
timeless

ly moon-a
wakening.

m) Kafka'

s light–open
ing door

depthed The
Lord's seclus

ive darkness
es.

n) Miss Black

burn erasing
that 2nd class

chalked-down
conspiring

guilt.

o) No-more-

witches be
witched those

darkly tidal
instinctual

desires.

p) Nothing-much-

left of her ap
pealing skin-

boned him to
those lost de

sires of
dream-intend

ing reverie
s.

a) Tropical

rain's soft
ly-sensed

skin-awaken
ing pleasur

able-reassur
ances.

b) He could

scarcely remem
ber her voiced-

down inescap
ably sound-

touched echo
ings.

c) Mendelssohn'

s lightly trans
parent scherzi

time–surfac
ings.

d) Impression

ism's form
lessly implied

shadowing
s.

e) Her hair'

s lighted–
touched scent–

persuasion
s.

f) Tiny bird'

s scarcely
fleeting

foot–stepp
ed sand–im

pression
s.

g) The spider'

s finely webb
ed decept

ively kept–
appearance

s.

h) Japanese

lithe woman'
s secretly

withhold
ing smiling

s.

i) Those tiny

white–dott
ed instinct

ual flower
ings.

Calusa's masked-souls (9)

a) Demonic

masks implor
ing the spirits–

of-the-dead'
s fear–resolv

ing distanc
es.

b) The masks

they've carved–
into the very

features of
their own

blood–line.

c) Masked-

theater
chanting live-

currents of
dead–admonish

ing truth
s.

d) Masking

as hide-and-
seek the en

dangered
ground–truth

s of self-sur
vival.

e) Those mask

ed–eyes star
ing through

timeless
ly spaced–

distanc
ings.

f) Calusian

eyes death-
masking time–

inhabiting
fear

s.

g) Masked-line

s chanting a
collective

ly communal
sourced–unity.

h) The soul

of watering
self–reflect

ive trans
ient inhabit

ings.

i) Those self

shadowing
s have per

haps left be
hind souled–

through appear
ances.

Calusian

mounds death-
inhabiting

untold spirit
ual height

s.

The Calusia

harvested
the sea's ti

dally-refresh
ing fish–

flows.

Are Indian

>spirits still
alive in the

>back-water
s of their

>soul's time
less wander

>ings.

When dream

>merges in
to the tidal

>flow of once
time-suspend

>ing reflect
ions.

Why Christ

>ianize a people
so deadly in

>tent on their
own identity

>life-claim
s.

a) Samuel Green'

s poems

at their best
word-ready

intent

b) where the in

visible poetry-
prose line

blurs into
time's still

receding
question

ings.

c) He can

voice me near
er than the

hesitant
touch of a

leathery
leaf

d) oft long-

reaching
sensed–con

text less
than hand–

confining.

What we did

n't do and
did–do two

times of
self–appar

ent truth
s.

On a mild

Floridian day
the sun full

with warmth–
time softly

spoken glad
nesses.

a) I'll poem

my own way
as the Calusia

shelled with
ornamental

sea-touched
origin

s.

b) A poem'

s catching
one's breath

to the night'
s mysterious

ly starred–
heaven

s.

Swimmer

s swelling
with tidal

sound-drift
ings.

Florida'

s "Fountain
s-of-youth"

aging with
misplaced

Midwestern
residue

s of Calu
sian pre-form

ing shell-
wound

s.

He plied the

seas with the
surety of a

fisherman'
s much-tried

fingers hold
ing a flash–

like momentary
fish-color

ings.

In imitation

Great poems
so move me

beyond the
spirit of my

own small-
palmed world

of silently
gleaming

stars.

Playing

cards wast
ing the time

away as if
death wasn'

t playing
cards with

them already.

a) Learning

from your
little child

knows more
of life than

you do by
not knowing

at all.

b) I don't

know what
critics know

but I know
more.

How much

money you've
raised America

n democracy
to a Bush-Clin

ton dynastic
plutocracy.

a) Some room

s remain but

voiceless
ly empty spa

ces valued
in yards–

and-feet.

b) Some doctor

s remain al
most faceless

ly distan
cing.

c) "What lake"

he responded
as St. Bernard

only to their
word's reflect

ionless intent.

d) In the sub

way the compu
ters all re

ceptively
alive eye-

glancing.

e) All day

they played–
at-card'

s hand-rang
ed to their

pulsed init
iative

s.

f) At my coll

ege interview
he also noted

eyes-down that
I played ping–

pong quite
well.

g) "Who are

you" she
asked as if

a name had
become his per

soned-being.

h) Even as

small children
they were ex

pected to
see less and

learn more.

i) Books be

came for her
nothing more

than a daily
assignment.

j) Viktor Frankl

even after Ausch
witz discover

ed man's spirit
which Freud had

left somewhere
down-deep in

the darkness
of our cellar

ed unbeing.

k) They built

skyscraper
s to shadow

those person
less being

s far-down
below.

l) What he re

membered
of the Vietnam

War was only
the daily

body-count.

m) "Love"

they used to
call it now

it's only
referred to

as "sex".

n) The Jews

had their
names taken

away cow—
burned to an

indelible
number.

o) When even

marriage has
become the

sacred bond
s of a pre—

arranged
caged—capti

vity.

a) When prose

did master
the poet's

mind—sense
left bare of

the soften
ing winds of

time's eter
nal flow.

b) Ode to Robert Frost

(for Corinne)

I may have
taken that o

ther road
long distanc

ing from your
s but I've

learned to
realize the

common-length
of your plain-

talked sense
we've lost so

much of long
times ago.

c) Don't ex

plain any
poem to me

haunting the
wind's chang

ing moods u
pon seas of

unrealized
time.

In Imitation

If you would
serve me dear

est Rosemarie
all-in-white

dressed-out
in nearest sym

pathies I
would prefer

butterfly-
leafed upon

such stead
ied pathed-

greenness
es.

The slim-

legged egret
thin-toed

his cautious
ways Beaked

with pene
trating

sharply dir
ected taste-

tender
s.

a) Poetical

ly adept when
the shape of

a word take
s-on its own

sound-sensed
meaning

s.

b) When the

silhouetting
shape of a

woman fully
satisfie

s his hand-
escorting

lip-defining
priorit

ies.

c) Calusian

wood carved
into its eye-

depthed va
cantly allur

ing obscurit
ies.

d) How have

these wingèd
aspiring

birds sky-
attuned spac

ious time-
flow.

a) The growth

of mangrove
trees from

the sea's
shallow-

rooted silen
ces.

b) When the

moon rises
through the

night's dark
ening shad

ows.

c) The ease

of the sea
turtle's

time–evok
ing distanc

ings.

d) Life bear

s witness to
its contin

ual birth-
timing

s.

e) Rosemarie

when your Calu
sa-haunting-

eyes shadow
my own light–

awareness
es.

f) Natural

life closer-
sensed to

The Lord's
eternal

time-echoing
s.

g) Listen

ing to the
depth of the

sea's with
holding si

lence
s.

h) On vain men-

of-science

when the
world's alive

with such in
visible unfath

omed myster
ies.

a) Pink cloth

ed his daily
self-respons

ive smiling
time's elus

ive coloring
s.

b) Aren't we

all masked in
routines of

self-decept
ive imagin

ings.

c) Chameleon

like politic
ian's "Trust

me" before they
start changing

their time-re
assuring atti

tudes.

d) Those Pontius

Pilate histor
ians reinter

preting what
was into the

other side of
otherwise

more so!

e) Pietist

s fearful
ly denying

their bodie'
s God-created

instinct
ual urging

s.

f) Or the Don

Juan's womanis
ing their in

bred fear of
self-unveiling

intimacie
s.

g) They built

a fortified
caste around

their self-
surround

ing person.

h) Don't

touch too
closely or

I'll recede
into my im

movable
shell.

i) I saw

her (or was
it the sha

dow of her)
clothed-in

impenetra
ble fear

s.

a) She alway

s defended
herself even

when she
shouldn't

as if that
impending

pain could
despite her

very-being.

b) That last-

minute-kind-of–
person alway

s catching–
up with his

untimely for
getfulness.

c) 2nd start

left her
through-phas

ing the tidal
depths of

those still
outlasting

currents of
the first.

d) Wife-mother-

teacher effi
ciently trans

fering the
apparent same

ness of each
as one–of–

three.

e) Border-

lined between
here and no

wheres–now
She inhabited

other people'
s needs for

helping her
out of their

such devast
ing self–re

appraisal
s.

f) Palm

shadowing
s their

self–attuning
silence

s.

g) What clitt

er–clatter of
her wood–peck

ered voicing
insidious

rumours of
those side–

glanced offer
ings.

a) Words I

can hear
half-deaf as

apparition
s of "once–

upon–a–time".

b) Calusa

like still on
the look-out

though smoke–
signals have

blown away
much of my

own sense-of–
remembrance.

a) Only after

the repeated
ground-beat

of his thought
s as dried-

out crutched-
wood.

b) The gladness

of your eye'
s subdued

sweetness
almost decora

tively intent.

c) Is taste

as a woman'
s sense-of-

dress inti
mately their

s or as a
fashion self-

responsive.

d) He placed

me where I
felt foreign–

estranged
Ezra Pound

(personae)
cold rock–sub

stancial
formed.

e) Why be im

pressed by ad
vanced degree

s when the
spirit remain

s substancial
ly samed.

f) Only when

the–child–in
us open–eye

currents of
sourced ori

gins.

g) Can we

really grammar
a person root

ed in the
fertile soil

of an ines
capable past.

h) That half-

moon's increa
sing bright

ness shadow
ed.

i) Or was it

our common
upstart re

sponse the
breakage

of replent
ishing soil.

Poetry books by David Jaffin

1. **Conformed to Stone,** Abelard-Schuman, New York 1968, London 1970.

2. **Emptied Spaces,** with an illustration by Jacques Lipschitz, Abelard-Schuman, London 1972.

3. **In the Glass of Winter,** Abelard-Schuman, London 1975, with an illustration by Mordechai Ardon.

4. **As One,** The Elizabeth Press, New Rochelle, N. Y. 1975.

5. **The Half of a Circle,** The Elizabeth Press, New Rochelle, N. Y. 1977.

6. **Space of,** The Elizabeth Press, New Rochelle, N. Y. 1978.

7. **Preceptions,** The Elizabeth Press, New Rochelle, N. Y. 1979.

8. **For the Finger's Want of Sound,** Shearsman Plymouth, England 1982.

9. **The Density for Color,** Shearsman Plymouth, England 1982.

10. **Selected Poems** with an illustration by Mordechai Ardon, English/Hebrew, Massada Publishers, Givatyim, Israel 1982.

11. **The Telling of Time,** Shearsman Books, Kentisbeare, England 2000 and Johannis, Lahr, Germany.

12. **That Sense for Meaning,** Shearsman Books, Kentisbeare, England 2001 and Johannis, Lahr, Germany.

13. **Into the timeless Deep,** Shearsman Books, Kentisbeare, England 2003 and Johannis, Lahr, Germany.

14. **A Birth in Seeing,** Shearsman Books, Exeter, England 2003 and Johannis, Lahr, Germany.

15. **Through Lost Silences,** Shearsman Books, Exeter, England 2003 and Johannis, Lahr, Germany.

16. **A voiced Awakening,** Shearsman Books, Exter, England 2004 and Johannis, Lahr, Germany.

17. **These Time-Shifting Thoughts**, Shearsman Books, Exeter, England 2005 and Johannis, Lahr, Germany.

18. **Intimacies of Sound,** Shearsman Books, Exeter, England 2005 and Johannis, Lahr, Germany.

19. **Dream Flow** with an illustration by Charles Seliger, Shearsman Books, Exeter, England 2006 and Johannis, Lahr, Germany.

20. **Sunstreams** with an illustration by Charles Seliger, Shearsman Books, Exeter, England 2007 and Johannis, Lahr, Germany.

21. **Thought Colors,** with an illustration by Charles Seliger, Shearsman Books, Exeter, England 2008 and Johannis, Lahr, Germany.

22. **Eye-Sensing,** Ahadada, Tokyo, Japan and Toronto, Canada 2008.

23. **Wind-phrasings,** with an illustration by Charles Seliger, Shearsman Books, Exeter, England 2009 and Johannis, Lahr, Germany.

24. **Time shadows,** with an illustration by Charles Seliger, Shearsman Books, Exeter, England 2009 and Johannis, Lahr, Germany.

25. **A World mapped-out,** with an illustration by Charles Seliger, Shearsman Books, Exeter, England 2010.

26. **Light Paths,** with an illustration by Charles Seliger, Shearsman Books, Exeter, England 2011 and Edition Wortschatz, Schwarzenfeld, Germany.

27. **Always Now,** with an illustration by Charles Seliger, Shearsman Books, Bristol, England 2012 and Edition Wortschatz, Schwarzenfeld, Germany.

28. **Labyrinthed,** with an illustration by Charles Seliger, Shearsman Books, Bristol, England 2012 and Edition Wortschatz, Schwarzenfeld, Germany.

29. **The Other Side of Self,** with an illustration by Charles Seliger, Shearsman Books, Bristol, England 2012 and Edition Wortschatz, Schwarzenfeld, Germany.

30. **Light Sources,** with an illustration by Charles Seliger, Shearsman Books, Bristol, England 2013 and Edition Wortschatz, Schwarzenfeld, Germany.

31. **Landing Rights,** with an illustration by Charles Seliger, Shearsman Books, Bristol, England 2014 and Edition Wortschatz, Schwarzenfeld, Germany.

32. **Listening to Silence,** with an illustration by Charles Seliger, Shearsman Books, Bristol, England 2014 and Edition Wortschatz, Schwarzenfeld, Germany.

33. **Taking Leave,** with an illustration by Mei Fêng, Shearsman Books, Bristol, England 2014 and Edition Wortschatz, Schwarzenfeld, Germany.

34. **Jewel Sensed,** with an illustration by Paul Klee, Shearsman Books, Bristol, England 2015 and Edition Wortschatz, Schwarzenfeld, Germany.

35. **Shadowing Images**, with an illustration by Pieter de Hooch, Shearsman Books, Bristol, England 2015 and Edition Wortschatz, Schwarzenfeld.

36. **Untouched Silences**, with an illustration by Paul Seehaus, Shearsman Books, Bristol, England 2016 and Edition Wortschatz, Schwarzenfeld.

37. **Soundlesss Impressions**, with an illustration by Qi Baishi, Shearsman Books, Bristol, England 2016 and Edition Wortschatz, Schwarzenfeld.

38. **Moon Flowers**, with a photograph by Hannelore Bäumler, Shearsman Books, Bristol, England 2017 and Edition Wortschatz, Schwarzenfeld.

39. **The Healing of a Broken World**, with a photograph by Hannelore Bäumler, Shearsman Books, Bristol, England 2018 and Edition Wortschatz, Cuxhaven.

40. **Opus 40**, with a photograph by Hannelore Bäumler, Shearsman Books, Bristol, England 2018 and Edition Wortschatz, Cuxhaven.

41. **Identity Cause**, with a photograph by Hannelore Bäumler, Shearsman Books, Bristol, England 2018 and Edition Wortschatz, Cuxhaven.

Book on David Jaffin's poetry: Warren Fulton, **Poemed on a beach,** Ahadada, Tokyo, Japan and Toronto, Canada 2010.